THE SEAS AND THEIR SHELLS

THE *SEAS* AND

Strombus (Euprotomus) listeri T. Gray.

THEIR *SHELLS*

A COLLECTOR'S GUIDE TO
THE SEASHELLS OF THE WORLD

SERGIO ANGELETTI

TRANSLATED FROM THE ITALIAN BY
JEAN RICHARDSON

DOUBLEDAY & COMPANY, INC.
GARDEN CITY, NEW YORK 1978

Published Originally Under the Title *I Mari e le Conchiglie*
by Longanesi & C., Milano

The photographs in this book were taken by:
ALDO BALLO, GIORGIO BARLETTA, CARLO BEVILACQUA, MARCO FERRARIO,
GIOVANNI PINNA, AND MARIO ROSIELLO

Designed by Laurence Alexander

Library of Congress Cataloging in Publication Data

Angeletti, Sergio.
  The seas and their shells.

  Translation of I mari e le conchiglie.
  Bibliography: p. 307.
  Includes index.
  1. Shells—Pictorial works. I. Title.
QL404.A5413   594'.04'7
ISBN: 0-385-01363-9
Library of Congress Catalog Card Number 77-74292

Copyright © 1973 by Longanesi & C., 20122 Milano, via Borghetto, 5
English Translation Copyright © 1978 by Doubleday & Company, Inc.

PREFACE TO THE FIRST, ITALIAN, EDITION

This is a book for people who enjoy the age-old pleasure of collecting shells and for the even greater number of people who are in love with the sea. We must all remember that we are dealing with a living world; that shells are only representatives of much more complex organisms that inhabit the sea; and that the sea itself is not a clichéd playground but a world to be explored without conquest, as we should by now know how to do.

THE SEAS AND THEIR SHELLS is a kind of tourist guide to the most important shells. It gives their location, origin, and mineral composition, and for those who want to study the subject seriously and don't just think of shells as idle souvenirs, it explains the latest techniques for finding, preserving, and forming a collection of them.

This book is the result not only of a life's work of research and compilation, but also of the many pleasurable personal experiences I have had in the field. This being the case, my conclusions are often subjective and open to discussion. I hope, nevertheless, that THE SEAS AND THEIR SHELLS will prove of value to all shell collectors; my one aim in writing it has been to produce a useful and instructive book.

THE AUTHOR

PREFACE TO THE SECOND, ANGLO-AMERICAN, EDITION

The first, Italian, edition of this book was published in December 1973. The author continued his revisions right up to press time, in an effort to make THE SEAS AND THEIR SHELLS truly up to date.

In scientific fields, however, four years constitute a very long period of time. New records, new data, new points of view, have rendered much of the information in the first edition obsolete, and the author felt that he could not allow his book to be translated without extensive revisions. This, therefore, is not merely a translation but a thoroughly revised and up-to-date Anglo-American edition.

THE AUTHOR

CONTENTS

PART 1   THE SHELLS

PART 2   THE SEAS

PART 3   COLLECTING SHELLS

REFERENCE NOTES

INDEX   317

INTRODUCTION

THE SEAS AND THEIR SHELLS is not merely an authoritative work of natural history; it is a clearly original, one could almost say personal, view of underwater life. The author does not address himself exclusively to seashell collectors; in fact he does not confine himself to seashells at all, however beautifully and completely they may be presented. His range is much wider, encompassing the basic principles of marine ecology and the study of the seas' fauna and their geographical distribution, as well as the techniques and methods used in setting up a shell collection.

The author has deliberately avoided mentioning the problem of pollution, not because he is unaware of its seriousness (how could he be?) or because he finds it easier to ignore it, for Professor Angeletti shares the concern felt by everyone today who truly cares about nature. He has, however, thought it preferable to issue here, at the beginning, a single, more powerful warning that may linger in the reader's mind as he or she progresses through the book. It is well known that the ecology of the sea is being seriously damaged by pollution and that whole communities of animals have practically disappeared in many areas. The result is that in many cases the study of the polluting forces has to a large extent displaced the study of zoology. The author has, rightly, I think, decided not to divert attention from the zoological or natural history aspect to that of the polluting factors, and this is the only time they will be mentioned.

It should be noted before passing on that the biological equilibrium and thus entire ecosystems have been seriously damaged by shell dealers, collectors, and overzealous keepers of aquariums. Thus it would not be fair to place all blame on industrial polluters.

The prime purpose of this book is to guide those interested in collecting seashells, and this it accomplishes exceedingly well. Most readers will be interested in the shells rather than in the animals themselves; a few will want to study dead marine creatures, while others will want to keep them live in aquariums. To all of these collectors THE SEAS AND THEIR SHELLS will come as a great boon. But once again, a word of caution. Given the peril many underwater species find themselves in today, the author would like to encourage collections of marine life photographs rather than collections of actual remains. Similarly, aquariums should be stocked with species able to reproduce in captivity rather than with species condemned by captivity to genetic oblivion.

Today we are beginning to doubt whether using living things as ornaments is a proper way to treat nature. Among the readers of this book, some no doubt will feel that, ethically and scientifically, it would be preferable to study living creatures without destroying them. To these readers THE SEAS AND THEIR SHELLS is especially dedicated.

PROFESSOR MENICO TORCHIO
Lecturer in Marine Biology at the University of Pavia

Editor's Note

We would like to thank Mr. Morris K. Jacobson,
of The American Museum of Natural History in New York,
for his invaluable editorial assistance.

NOTE ON THE ILLUSTRATIONS

The captions in this book have been presented in abbreviated form. For example, the phrase "A shell of . . ." has not been repeated for each plate. We have also used the style "from 5 to 45 m," in most cases omitting the words "at a depth of." The arrows between one geographical location and another mean "to" or "as far as." They thus trace a line indicating the distribution area of each animal concerned. Parentheses around a geographical area indicate unconfirmed or poorly confirmed recordings. The captions will be clearer after you have read the sections "Zoning" (*p. 37*) and "Systematic Notes" (*p. 19*).

THE SEAS AND THEIR SHELLS

PART 1

The Shells

WHAT THEY ARE, WHAT MAKES THEM

Anyone who collects shells is actually collecting skeletons. Shells are often thought of in nursery rhymes as "houses," but their primary function is to act as mechanical organs supporting the bulk of the shell-bearer's muscles. In other words, they are skeletons: more precisely, exoskeletons, a term that refers not only to their position but also to their origin. Shells are formed by the action of the shell-bearer's uppermost, or cutaneous, layer of cells, and not, as in the more familiar case of man and all other vertebrates, by mesenchymal tissues within the organism.

Skeletons are characteristically hard, and shells are the hardest of skeletons. The majority of them have a very high percentage (on the average 94 per cent) of calcium carbonate, the fundamental component of limestone and marble.

Among the creatures endowed with a hard, impenetrable exterior, the mollusks (clams, snails, squids, and so on) are perhaps the most familiar, if only for gastronomic reasons. The rest of the shell-bearers,[1] a heterogeneous group of animals, are little known outside scientific circles: among these are the brachiopods, which are only superficially similar to the mollusks; certain crustaceans such as the Ostracoda, Conchostraca, and Cirripedia; and certain sedentary polychaetes of the annelid worms phylum.[2] But only the shells of the mollusks and, occasionally, of the brachiopods are of any general interest.

[1] *"Shell-bearer" is used here in the broad sense of every animal whose skeleton is a shell.*

[2] *Of which the* Serpula *and the* Spirorbis *are perhaps the best known to the layperson, as they are often exhibited in marine aquaria.*

Mollusks

The mollusks, which include more than 127,000 (mostly marine) species are the second largest group of homogeneous animals, after the insects. They are also the most isolated group in the zoological world: only the most ancient links are discernible between mollusks and any other group.

For a long time the earliest fossil evidence of mollusks consisted of fragments of shells that had undoubtedly belonged to gastropods (*see p. 8*) but could not be more specifically identified. These were found in the 550-million-year-old geological strata of the Colorado Algonkian. In May 1973, however, the fossil of a bivalve (*see p. 13*), *Fordilla troyensis Barrande*, which had been brought to the surface in 1881 at Troy, New York, was recognized as dating from at least 570 million years ago. But if one takes into account the fact that the earliest known mollusks are already very well defined and complex organisms, then the story of their evolution must have begun much earlier, at least twice as far back as has been supposed, i.e., more than a billion years ago.

According to the most logical theories put forward in recent years, the first mollusks must have inhabited the lower midlittoral or sublittoral zones (*see pp. 40–41*) of the continental shelf, where in turn they originated from the same mass of Turbellaria/Nemertina worms as did the first arthropods and annelids.[3]

The first mollusk, in order to merit the name, must have differed noticeably from its probable, but still hypothetical, "worm" ancestors, by having created for itself three characteristic structures: a muscular sole (the *foot*), which it needed to move; a *visceral sac*, which contained its inner organs of respiration, circulation, digestion, excretion, and reproduction; and a double fold of skin (the *mantle* or *pallium*), which had various functions, including the production of the shell. To explain how the anatomy of a worm became that of a mollusk without involving the kind of drastic changes and leaps forward that nature never makes, one must imagine the starting point as a gradual change in eating habits accompanied by the adaptation and transformation of the digestive

---

[3] *These groups of animals are characterized by egg cells that divide along a spiral axis. They make up more than 90 per cent of living animals.*

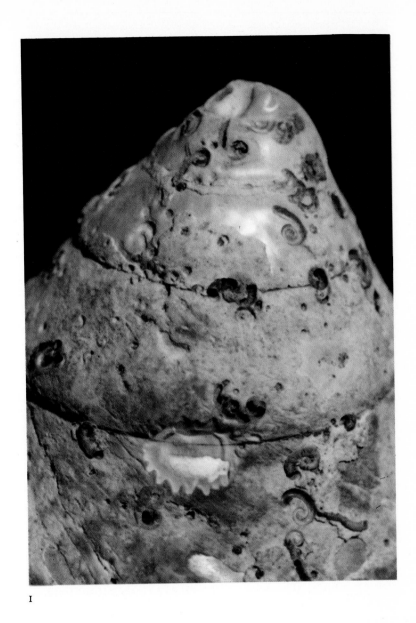

I

1. Initial whorls of the *Tectus niloticus* L., a mother-of-pearl species found from southern Japan→the Philippines→ Australia and New Caledonia. This specimen shows signs of intense marine life (×2½).

system, whereby, over a long period, the thickening of the cells led to the development of a digestive tube and its associated glands. The growth of this internal mass stimulated the ventral muscles in the lower part of the body to become stronger and harder in order to balance and support the added weight of the digestive tract (a process culminating in the formation of the foot), while on the back of the body, to make room for the new organs, a visceral hump (the visceral sac) formed; finally, as a measure of protection, the skin became folded and hardened by absorbing limestone substances in its environment, thus forming the mantle and eventually the shell.

Whether the evolutionary sequence occurred in this manner or somewhat differently, a common structural scheme, based on the trio *foot—visceral sac—mantle* (shell), is readily evident in all the many different forms mollusks have attained over the centuries.[4]

For study purposes, the group of mollusks (phylum Mollusca) can be divided into two subphyla: (1) the Aculifera, which lack true shells and consist of three classes: the Solenogastres, the Caudofoveata,[5] and the Polyplacophora; and (2) the shell-bearing Conchifera, which are subdivided into five classes: the Tryblidiacea (also called Monoplacophora), the Gastropoda (gastropods), the Scaphopoda (scaphopods), the Bivalvia (bivalves), and the Cephalopoda (cephalopods).

The Aculifera, which include some 1,200 species in all, seem like survivors from an evolutionary stage surpassed for the most part by other mollusks. They have a wormlike body and a functional anatomy that seems clumsy: their tentacles, visual organs, and sense of balance are all developed to a lesser degree than in the Conchifera. This is particularly true of the Solenogastres and Caudofoveata, which instead of a shell have a kind of extended cuticle reinforced by limestone particles (spicules) embedded in it. The Polyplacophora bear what is known as a *lorica* rather than a shell— a loose arrangement of eight transverse limestone plates joined like tiles forming a roof.

---

[4] *It is customary to quote J. F. Correa, who in 1806 was among the first to see in the structure of the mollusks a basic theme "tenaciously followed but richly varied."*

[5] *The Caudofoveata and the Solenogastres are often grouped together under the name Aplacophora.*

On the whole the Aculifera, with the possible exception of the Polyplacophora class, have not been the subject of a comprehensive study, and therefore our knowledge of them is spotty.[6] Although they are mollusks, the fact that the Aculifera do not have true shells excludes them from further consideration here.

The most popular mollusk species are found in the subphylum Conchifera, which includes all the shelled mollusks and those lacking true shells but descended from shell-bearing ancestors.

It is these mollusks which have been, biologically, the most successful and versatile. They range in size from a millimeter to twenty-two meters long, are found in the sea, in fresh water, and on land, can be either attached to substrata or free-moving, confined to certain areas or cosmopolitan, "as stupid as an oyster" or endowed with the almost human intelligence of an octopus, and, above all, they produce tens of thousands of wonderful shells.

One has only to look at the great variety of these limestone skeletons to realize how versatile shelled mollusks have been in the course of their evolution, and how fruitful has been the flexibility with which they have countered the severe restrictions of natural selection.

As mentioned before, concrete evidence and reasonable deductions all indicate that mollusks have nearly always lived in large numbers in the sea. There the currents, changing but never ceasing through the years, scattered mollusk larvae throughout the globe, inducing the species to modify themselves, to produce what at their level was the right animal at the right moment in the right place.

And protected by the right shell: the fantastic forms and splendid colors have a purpose exceeding their aesthetic value, a purpose indicated by the shell-bearers' antiquity, by their efficiency as "biological machines," and by their adaptability in the face of events that are now long passed, but that have inevitably marked them.

In many respects the TRYBLIDIACEA are the exceptions that confirm the established theories on shells. Until 1958 they were found

---

[6] However, this ought not to be the case, as there is much of interest in this group. A solenogaster Strophomenia indica (Nierstrasz) has been recorded and studied in Indonesia and in the Gulf of Naples.

only in paleontological texts, grouped with the gastropod fossils. They are, in fact, another example of a "living fossil": they were already on earth in the Cambrian period, half a billion years ago, and were thought to have become extinct in the Silurian period, that is, about 350 million years ago.

But on 6 May 1952 the Danish laboratory ship *Galathea* dredged up from a depth of 3,570 meters off the coast of Costa Rica the first ten complete specimens plus three empty shells of an animal with a saucer-shaped, or patelliform, shell, 5 cm in diameter, which was identified only some years later (in 1957) as a living tryblidiacean and given the name *Neopilina galatheae* Lemche. Since then, fresh discoveries have followed fairly frequently, confirming that the Tryblidiacea have survived unchanged, are widely distributed, and are not just an accidental phenomenon. In 1958 *Neopilina (Vema) ewingi* Clarke and Menzies was found between 5,611 and 6,324 meters in the Peru-Chile Trench; in 1960 *Neopilina veleronis* Menzies and Layton was found off the California peninsula; *Neopilina bruuni* and *Neopilina bacescui* were collected by Menzies, again in the Peru-Chile Trench, in 1967; and on 22 February of the same year came the first discovery of a tryblidiacean in the waters of the Old World, when the subspecies *Neopilina galatheae adenensis* Tebble was dredged up from a depth of 3,950 meters in the Gulf of Aden.

The discovery of living Tryblidiacea has not only shaken the very roots of the mollusks' genealogical tree, causing a reassessment of their whole classification, but has also made clear once and for all that in the depths of the oceans there are frontiers both between different periods and between different biotic environments. The *Neopilina*, however, are of little importance to shell collectors, because of their rather humble appearance and because they are not found above depths of 2,500 meters.

With 105,000 species, almost all of which are shelled and 69,000 of which are marine, the GASTROPODS constitute the largest class of all shell-bearing animals. It is the gastropods' shell that instinctively comes to mind at the mention of the word *seashell* and it is to this type of shell that we turn for the sound of the sea.

The wide range of forms that the size and diversity of the phylum Mollusca would lead one to expect is nowhere more evident than in the shells of the gastropods. These are all of one piece (univalve) and usually conical. They can either have a fairly wide base, as do the limpets, or be very elongated and rather tubiform. The latter type includes shells that are either asymmetrically coiled on themselves (*see Figs. 38 and 112*), or—and this is the more common configuration—coiled symmetrically in a spiral extending into space like a screw.

The beginning, or tip, of the spiral is called the *apex*, and the opening at its end is called the *aperture*. If, when you hold a shell with its apex upward, the aperture, facing you, is on the right, the shell is said to be *dextral*. Most shells fall into this category. If the aperture is seen on the left, as it is in a small number of species (*see Fig. 118*) or through some abnormality, the shell is said to be *sinistral*.

In both cases the spiral is centered around a precise geometric axis in the form of an axial pillar called the *columella*. The coilings,

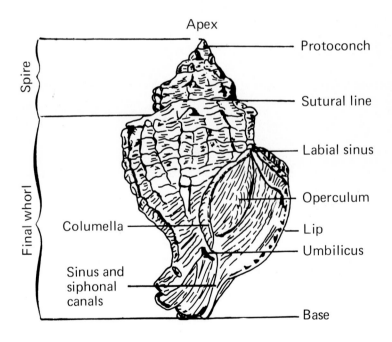

Diagram of a gastropod shell.

2–3. Dorsal section of a cowrie shell (*see Fig. 141*) and a view from the left side of a trumpet (*see Fig. 63*): note the columellae (*see p. 9*) and the balanced architectural layout, which is not apparent from the outside because the body whorl encloses all the others (×1⅓ and 1¼).

or *whorls*, around the axis are known collectively as the *spire*. This is made up of the *protoconch*, which is the earliest, embryonic part of the shell and usually corresponds to the apex; the various *whorls*, or coils; and the *suture*, which is the spiral line where the whorls meet. Beneath the spire of a gastropod shell is the *body whorl*, which consists of the *aperture*, the largest opening of the shell; the *dorsum*, or back, opposite the aperture; and the *base*, which is the part of the shell opposite the apex. Frequently there is a depression of varying size at the center of the base of the body whorl, beneath the columella, called the *umbilicus*. The rim that runs practically all around the aperture is called the lip, or *peristome*; its outer edge is called the *labrum*, and its inner edge, the *labium*. The *operculum* is a separate calcareous structure made by and attached to the fleshy part of some gastropods. Its primary purpose is to close the aperture of the shell when the rest of the creature has drawn itself into it.

In addition to these basic parts there is the whole series of extra, "corrective" elements that differentiate the various species. These include the wide variety of colors and designs; the "carved" markings on the surface of the shell, within the aperture, and around the peristome; and such structures as the *siphonal canal* and the *labial sinus* (grooves opening from the aperture toward the base and the apex respectively) and the extensions of the labrum, which can be either winged (*see Frontispiece and Figs. 122, 125, 216,*

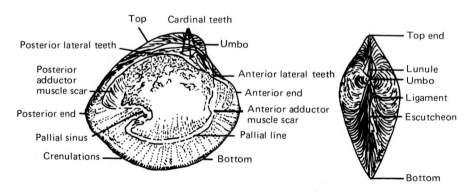

Diagram of a Bivalve shell.

250), foliaceous (*see Figs. 202 and 247*), or digitated (*see Figs. 137, 139, 160, 161, 162, 163, 222*).

The univalve shells of the SCAPHOPODS tend to have very little ornamentation: simply a series of narrow and protruding, ribbed axial markings. In all there are 350 scaphopod species, all marine, and they are second only to the Tryblidiacea in the paucity of shell variations. The scaphopod's shell is open at both ends, tubiform, and, to various degrees, curved and tapering.[7] Its concave side corresponds to the dorsal region and its lesser opening marks the posterior of the shell, which is sometimes accompanied by incisions, clefts, and small holes.

The shells of the approximately 20,000 species of BIVALVES (three quarters of which are marine) are usually composed of two symmetrical pieces, the *valves*, joined to form a powder-compact-like "container."

It is nearly always possible to see concentric bands on the exterior surface of the bivalves (this does not hold true for any other shell group). These bands correspond to the *lines of growth*, and at the beginning of the progression of these lines on each valve are situated the *umbones*, embryonic vestiges that mark the upper (dorsal) area of the shell. Here, too, is located the *hinge* joining the two valves, which consists of an *elastic ligament* and a varying complex of teeth, thin plates, and indentations. Inside the shell one can see the *scars* where the *adductor muscles* were inserted; there can be either one or two adductor muscles, raised or sunken, identical or different. Springing from the adductor muscles and running parallel to the edge is the *pallial line*, actually a scar along the inner surface of a bivalve shell marking the line of attachment of the shell-producing *mantle*. The pallial line often has an indentation called the *pallial sinus*, which always marks the posterior of the shell, as does the adductor muscle scar if there is only one such muscle; if there are two adductor muscles and one is significantly larger than the other, then the larger marks the posterior. Showy colors and rather elaborate sculptural decorations are sometimes found on bivalve shells, but these are not common.

[7] *Like an elephant's tusk.*

The great majority of CEPHALOPODS no longer have shells. Of about 730 species living in the sea, cuttlefish and squids have only an internal and greatly modified shell in the form of the cuttlebone and the pen; only four species have a fairly normal shell. Three of these belong to the genus *Nautilus* (*see Figs. 206, 207, 208*) and one to the genus *Spirula* (*see Fig. 12*). The *Argonauta* is a case apart among the cephalopods.

In the shelled species of the *Nautilus* and *Spirula* cephalopods, we have a type of univalve shell that coils around the middle plane of the body and is divided by a progressive series of partitions (or *septa*) into a number of distinct *chambers* (*see Fig. 4*). While the other chambers are for the most part filled with nitrogen, the largest and most recently produced chamber of the *Nautilus* shell houses the fleshy parts of the creature. In the *Spirula*, on the other hand, the fleshy part surrounds practically the entire shell.

Thanks to a siphuncle (a tubular connection) that runs through the septa, the *Nautilus* and the *Spirula* are able to vary the volume of gas in their chambers, thus providing a precise hydrostatic system used for vertical underwater navigation.[8]

Finally, only the females of the genus *Argonauta* (*see Figs. 106 and 178*) have a shell, but it is unlike that of any other mollusk. The *Argonauta* shell is not produced by the mantle but by the expansion of two special tentacles; it does not serve as a skeleton but is periodically and spontaneously cast off, to serve as a nest for newly laid eggs. During this period of incubation, a new shell is generated.

AN ANALYSIS OF THE CHEMICAL STRUCTURE
OF MOLLUSK SHELLS

Chemical examination reveals that the majority of mollusk shells are composed of calcium carbonate (89 to 99 per cent) in its three

[8] *The name* Nautilus *was introduced by Linnaeus in 1758. A hundred years later, Jules Verne (1828–1905) borrowed the name for his submarine commanded by Captain Nemo. But before this, in 1801, Robert Fulton had given it to a torpedo-shaped, single-seater, submersible boat which he had invented. A second real-life* Nautilus *appeared in 1886, an "immersion" boat invented by Andrew Campbell and James Ash that was immersed by means of large pumps that took on enough water to submerge the boat and keep it under control under water.* Nautilus *was also the name given to the first nuclear submarine, launched by the U. S. Navy in 1955.*

4

4. X ray of a nautilus shell (*see p. 14 and Fig. 208*), showing the logarithmic spiral layout and the series of chambers with the segments of the siphuncle that provides communication between them ($\times\frac{2}{3}$).

crystalline forms: trigonal *calcite*, orthorhombic *aragonite*, and hexagonal *vaterite*. The remaining percentage consists of small amounts of tricalcium phosphate, silicon, calcium sulfate, magnesium carbonate, ferric oxide, phosphorus trioxide, and finally a proportionally minute amount of organic material consisting of the polysaccharide *conchiolin*, a scleroprotein[9] responsible for holding the entire shell fabric together.

All of this shell material is usually deposited in three layers of varying thicknesses: the outermost is the *periostracum*, which has the highest organic content and protects the more mineralized layers underneath from wear and chemical erosion; the middle layer, the *prismatic* (ostracum), consists of columnar microcrystals rhythmically arranged in varying patterns and angularities; in the innermost layer (hypostracum) the microcrystals are lamellar and foliated. This last layer is called *calcitostracum* if it is made of calcite or *nacreous* (mother of pearl)[10] if it is made of aragonite.

Brachiopods

Brachiopod fossil remains (*Lingulella*) can be dated back nearly one billion years. The brachiopods have changed very little in the course of that time span, except that the number of species has dwindled from the 7,000 of the Devonian period to the 260 marine species of today. Brachiopods (Brachiopoda) are classified in the phylum Tentaculata. They have been at something of a disadvantage in the eyes of collectors because of their external similarity to bivalve mollusks, with which they have long been confused and to which one always refers in describing them. The brachiopods have as a protective skeleton a bivalve shell composed of calcium and magnesium carbonates, calcium phosphate, and chitin depos-

---

[9] *Akin to that found in fingernails, in the elytra of beetles, and in the carapaces of crabs.*

[10] *The characteristic nacreous shine is caused by refraction of the light through the many transparent plates of the microcrystals, a light effect well known in optics.*

ited in three layers. There are two major differences between brachiopods and bivalve mollusks: (1) the brachiopod shell is oriented along the dorsal-ventral rather than the lateral body axis; and (2) in addition to their shells, brachiopods have internal skeletal pieces (the *lophophore* with the *brachidium; see Fig. 67*).

The class Brachiopoda is divided into two orders: the ecardines and the testicardines. The former have symmetrical valves without a hinge, while the latter are characterized by asymmetrical hinged valves. (In this case, the ventral valve is concave, larger and wider than the dorsal.) The brachiopods are found in practically all seas from the lower midlittoral zone to the abyssal zone. This statement is admittedly vague, but in fact brachiopods have been found wherever a specific search for them has been carried out, but such a search has not occurred everywhere.

SYSTEMATIC NOTES

There is a dynamic, flowing quality in the continual evolution of the world of biology that results in a great variety of phenomena. The individuals bound up in such cosmic variability become unique, each one different from all the others. Thus any attempt to systematize these creatures is bound to be arbitrary and artificial.

Life itself cannot be scientifically analyzed or described in simple terms; the life sciences do not approach the physical sciences in preciseness; they have no basic formulas that can be deduced step by step. However, the methods of human learning—which were decisively shaped in late Neolithic times, about 7,000 years ago— enable us to distinguish and to classify large numbers of facts in an orderly fashion, and this ability to classify underlies every branch of knowledge.

Zoological classification is not as fixed as, for example, Mendeleev's arrangement of the elements, since it takes place in the face of slow but continual evolution and change. In spite of this, a system of arranging and naming vast numbers of organisms has been set up, based upon several generally accepted conventions. These conventions we shall now summarize, paying particular attention

ON THE FOLLOWING PAGES:

5–6. *Columbella rustica* (L.), a very common species in the Mediterranean and the Atlantic from Portugal→Madeira, the Canaries, the Azores, and Guinea; widely scattered and exceptionally abundant on littoral algae. The specimen on the right is mature, with a narrow opening and typical serration; the other, with rather different peristomial characteristics (*see p. 12*), is simply a young, immature specimen ($\times 13$ and $\times 10$).

to the problem of nomenclature,[1] which is often so troublesome to the nonspecialist.

Animals that can interbreed and produce viable and fertile offspring are called a *species*, closely related species form a *genus*, a number of related genera form a *family*, and so on through *orders, classes, phyla,* and *kingdoms*. This arrangement is based upon human evaluation, often very subjective, and hence specialists in a single group are not always in agreement on the delineation of species, genera, families, and so on. To ease this situation, a system of intermediate points has also been set up so that there are kingdoms and subkingdoms; superphyla, phyla, and subphyla; superclasses, classes, and subclasses; superorders, orders, and suborders; superfamilies, families, and subfamilies; tribes and subtribes; genera and subgenera; superspecies, species, and subspecies; and also forms and varieties.

The following rules of nomenclature apply to the vast number of scientific names now in existence:

—Single names are used for subgenera and all groups above them, two names for the species, and three names for the subspecies.
—Latin or latinized names are used, and those of nonclassical origin are treated grammatically as though they were Latin.
—Names from subgenus upward are written with a capitalized initial letter.
—The single generic name is treated like a substantive (noun) in the nominative singular case.
—When a genus is divided into subgenera, the typical subgenus (also called the nominal subgenus) bears the same name as the genus; the subgeneric name is written in parentheses between the generic and specific names.

---

[1] *There is some confusion about the use of the terms* classification, systematics, taxonomy, *and* nomenclature. *These are often incorrectly treated as synonyms.* Classification *originally meant the placing of objects into classes according to a basic plan;* systematics *referred to the theory underlying such an organization, and* nomenclature *to the assigning of names to the units of such groupings.* Taxonomy, *although introduced long ago, came into general use only recently with a vaguer meaning, including certain aspects of the other three. This has caused even more confusion.*

—The names of the species and subspecies are written (always in that order) in lowercase letters. Both agree grammatically with the generic name.

—The *author* of a scientific name is the person who first published it with a definition or description; this name is written after the scientific name.

—When, after revision, a species is placed in a different genus from the original one, the name of the author of the specific name is retained, but it is put into parentheses.

—This system of nomenclature in zoology began with the tenth edition of Linnaeus' *Systema Naturae* (1758); thus this date is taken as the point of departure in matters of priority among authors.

Following are some examples: Linnaeus[2] designated the most common Mediterranean limpet *Patella caerulea* L. (*see Fig. 13*), and it retained this name through many revisions. In 1789 Gmelin introduced a new species in the genus *Patella* and called it *ferruginea*, thus producing the name *Patella ferruginea* Gmelin. In 1884 Monterosato set up a subgenus in the genus *Patella*, naming it *Patellastra*, to which Gmelin's *-ferruginea* belonged. Thus we have *Patella* (*Patellastra*) *ferruginea* Gmelin (*see Fig. 14*); and the earlier *-caerulea* L., which remained in the nominal subgenus, became *Patella* (*Patella*) *caerulea* L.[3]

The species that appeared as *Cypraea lurida* L. in Linnaeus' 1758 classification was placed by Jousseaume in 1884 in the genus *Luria*, thus becoming *Luria lurida* (L.). But since the genus *Luria* had been divided into subgenera, and the species *lurida* had subspecies, the full name of Linnaeus' species is written *Luria* (*Luria*) *lurida lurida* (L.) (*see Fig. 48*).

As older works are examined more critically, it is often discovered that the same species has been named more than once by

[2] *Since the name Linnaeus is so widely known, it is customarily abbreviated to "L.," as it is in this book.*

[3] *This repetition of the generic name as a subgeneric name merely indicates that the genus has been divided into one or more subgenera. The subgeneric name is used regularly only when it differs from the generic name.*

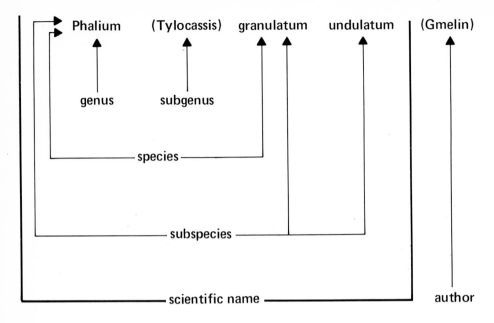

The composition of a scientific name.

different authors. In this case the earliest most precise and descriptive name is considered the correct one. Thus the name *Natica millepunctata* (Lamarck) 1810 has been superseded by *Naticarius stercusmuscarum* (Gmelin) 1792 (*see Fig. 71*).

Bibliographical research also reveals an occasional misattribution: i.e., a systematic work ascribed to a certain scholar is actually the result of another's research. Thus several revised authoritative works now reflect the new authorships. For instance, *Conus (Rhizoconus) mustelinus* Bruguière in the work entitled *Tableaux . . . des Trois Regnes de la Nature* (1792) became *Conus (Rhizoconus) mustelinus* Hwass in Bruguière (*see Fig. 158*), and *Nautilus scrobiculatus* Solander in *A Catalogue of the Portland Museum*

(1786) was changed to *Nautilus scrobiculatus* Lightfoot (*see Fig. 207*). It is clear that such changes occur as new facts are discovered and work updated—often almost as soon as a new species is described and named.[4]

---

[4] *It is worth pointing out again that nature was not made to be classified. It is presumptuous to expect it to adapt itself to schemes that exist only in the mind of one of its latest creations.*

PART 2

The Seas

THE TETHYS SEA

Four and a half billion years ago there was no water on the earth. The process of cooling and consolidating was just reaching the stage that allowed a somewhat durable crust to form. This crust consisted mainly of components already stable at high temperatures, such as silicides, hydrides, and carbides, which were formed by the union of various metals with silicon, hydrogen, and carbon. These were followed by the appearance of the oxides: combinations of various metals with oxygen, which also united with nitrogen, sulfur, and phosphorus to form nitrates, sulfates, and phosphates.

But there was still no water. Before this vital element could form, the primeval environment of the earth, during the following billion years, had to reach the point at which hydrogen[1] could react with the ferric oxides to form water vapor. This vapor began to condense in the sky and on the earth: as it evaporated from below, it rained from above.

It rained for at least 500 million years. The water that fell on the newly emerged continents fiercely eroded them. Thus the first sedimentary rocks were formed and the sea water acquired its salt. The oceans appeared on earth 3,700,000 years ago and differed from the oceans of today not only in geographical configuration, but, most importantly, in the absence of life. Very soon after the formation of the oceans, however, life did appear, and without much difficulty since the conditions favoring its development were all present. As a matter of fact, the first fossil remains of single or grouped algae date from about 3,700,000 years ago.

Shell-bearing fossils date from a much later period, but these are already so highly developed as to indicate a considerably earlier point of origin. Hence, shell-bearing animals had plenty of time to

[1] *Etymologically* hydrogen *means "the creator of water."*

7

7. *Quibulla ampulla* (L.), throughout the Indo-Pacific from East Africa→southern Japan→the southern Pacific islands and northeastern Australia, and *Bulla striata* (Bruguière), from the Mediterranean and the Atlantic as far as the Azores, the Antilles, and the Bahamas; both are common at the bottom of fields of algae ($\times 2\frac{3}{4}$).

8. *Mitra papalis* L., in the Indo-Pacific from East Africa→ southern Japan→Micronesia, common on sand at the base of rocks, in the sublittoral zone down to 20 m; and *Mitra (Nebularia) belcheri* Hinds, in the American Pacific from Magdalena Bay→ (Gulf of California)→Panama, fairly common in circumlittoral zone at 40 m and below ($\times 1\frac{1}{3}$).

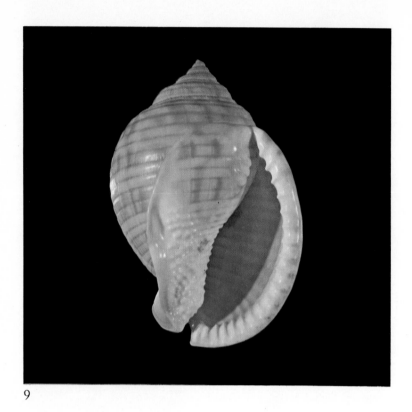

9

9. *Phalium* (*Tylocassis*) *granulatum undulatum* (Gmelin), a subspecies of the Mediterranean and the Atlantic as far as the Azores, Madeira, and the Canary Islands, closely related to *P. granulatum granulatum* (Born), of the American Atlantic from North Carolina→Bermuda→Bahia (Brazil), and, on the other side of Panama, in the American Pacific, *P. granulatum centiquadratum* (Valenciennes), from Mexico to Peru; common in sandy sublittoral zone (×1).

10

10. *Harpa crenata* Swainson, in the American Pacific from
Magdalena Bay→Gulf of California→Gorgona Island
(Colombia), the only American species of a group widely
scattered in the Indo-Pacific (*see Figs. 177 and 180*); but
Harpa ventricosa Lamarck (on the right) is found only along
the East African coast, from the Red Sea→Natal and as far
as Madagascar→the Seychelles→Mauritius. The latter is
fairly common in midlittoral zone to 5 m, the former in
sublittoral zone to 45 m (×⅚).

spread throughout the seas.[2] If we want to understand their distribution today, we will have to go back as far as possible, back to the time when an immense ocean stretched across the greater part of our planet in a generally east-west direction. It united the eastern Pacific, the central Atlantic, the Mediterranean, the Indian Ocean, and the western Pacific, and divided the continental masses into two main groups, one in the north and one in the south. Both Central America and southwest Asia were then under water. This sea has been called the Mediterranic, the Mesozoic Mediterranean, the Sea of Nummulites,[3] the Mesogée, or—commemorating the wife of the sea god Oceanus—the Tethys Sea. All paleogeographers agree that it did indeed exist but differ on its exact dimensions, the time of its appearance, and its duration. At any rate, the Tethys Sea was one of the most constant and essential features of the earth's topography throughout long geological periods. It was already in existence in the Lower Cambrian (600 million years ago) and, aside from some local interruptions, it lasted until the Late Tertiary, at the threshold of the Pleistocene, when man first appeared.

Of importance here is the development of the Tethys Sea during the 200 million years comprising the Mesozoic plus the first stages of the Tertiary. Geologic marine deposits in the Mediterranean and southwest Asian regions show many signs of the great extent of this ancient link between the Atlantic and Indian oceans. Thus during this entire period the marine fauna of the Indian Ocean, the western Pacific, the Mediterranean, the tropical Atlantic, and eastern Pacific were, within the limits of such a vast expanse, part of a single major unit, the fauna of the Tethys Sea. This situation was profoundly altered by two fundamental events that occurred in the Miocene and Pliocene periods (30 to 15 million years ago).[4]

[2] *As well as onto the land and into fresh water.*

[3] *Nummulites are fossil Foraminifera.*

[4] *It should be remembered that almost the whole of the Tertiary was a period of vast orogenetic (mountain-building) movements. The most important of these was the great earth folding of the continental land mass between Eurasia to the north and Africa and southern Asia to the south, which led to the rise of the Alps, the Pyrenees, the Atlas Mountains, the Carpathians, the Caucasus, and the Himalayas (where marine deposits have been found at heights of more than 7,000 meters). In the Americas the Rockies and the Andes also appeared at this time.*

These were the formation of the Isthmus of Panama between the two Americas and the emergence of an arm of land, southwest Asia, between Asia and Africa. This put an end to the Tethys Sea as a single ocean, and the four oceans we know today (the Arctic, Atlantic, Pacific, and Indian) appeared in outline.

More or less at the same time, extensive climatic changes took place. These resulted in a drastic lowering of the temperature, which particularly affected the Atlantic environment and caused the larger part of the western Atlantic fauna to lose its Indo-Pacific characteristics. The region also became much poorer in the number of species.

Thus the marine zoogeographical situation of today reflects the contrast between the fauna of the Indo-(western) Pacific and that of the Atlantic-(eastern) Pacific. Subsequently these two types developed along very different lines.

ZONING

Nature is not a show at which we are only spectators. It is a drama in which we are not merely actors but actual characters, deeply involved in the plot. Yet it is apparent that no one can be a scientist without at least pretending to be a spectator, for a better view of the action and the scenery of the play. The sea has certainly not escaped the human need to classify what is being studied. It has been subdivided into various zones, provinces, and regions, each merging into others to form a single whole, but each with its own characteristics, which must be understood in order to comprehend the whole.

First there is the *coastal zone* where the dry and watery worlds meet. The boundary where the coast sinks into the sea and the sea bathes it with its waves and tides is called the *coastline*. It is closely identified with the *tidal* or *intertidal zone* which is the area between the maximum and minimum levels of high and low tide. From here the sea bottom slopes more or less gently down to a depth of between 120 and 350 meters and forms a submerged declivity called the *continental shelf* all around the dry land. At the edge of this, at a mean depth of 200 meters, the drop increases sharply, forming a kind of step, called the *talus*, with a *bathyal slope* that runs down to 1,500 to 3,000 meters. At this level begins the *abyssal* shelf, which, with its own fairly gentle slope, can reach a depth of up to 6,000 meters. Beyond this limit lies the *hadal zone*, which extends down to the greatest depths known.

The waters that cover the continental shelf are called *epicontinental* and form the *neritic province*, while the *oceanic province* includes all the waters beyond the talus. From a more strictly biological point of view the seabed from the coasts to the abyss is called the *benthic domain*, while the open sea forms the *pelagic domain*, which in turn is subdivided into the *epipelagic domain* (from the surface down to the level of the talus), the *bathypelagic* (corresponding in depth to the slope of the talus), the *abyssopelagic* (from 3,000 to 6,000 meters, above the abyssal shelf), and the *hadal region* beyond.

The marine biologic world is therefore divided into benthic and pelagic species. The former live in close contact with the bottom and are either fixed or mobile, but never travel very far from the bottom or for a very long period of time; the latter live in the open sea, from the surface down to varying depths, have no lasting contact with the bottom, and are not directly dependent on it or its inhabitants for food. Pelagic species can be either *planktonic*, i.e., incapable of any independent movement and carried in suspension by the waters, or *nektonic*, i.e., capable of independent movement.

As we have said, these are synthetic divisions acting as "frames" in which the animal (and vegetable) marine populations appear to live, though they do make frequent, systematic changes from one "frame" to another. Not all the organisms considered planktonic remain in that state all their lives. Some mainly benthic groups such as the annelids, crustaceans, and mollusks are planktonic in the first stages of their development but cease to be so as they reach maturity and head for the seabed. The amount of fish and molluscan life present in the nekton of the coastal waters varies according to seasonal, periodical, or even sudden and unexplained migrations from and to the littoral zone.

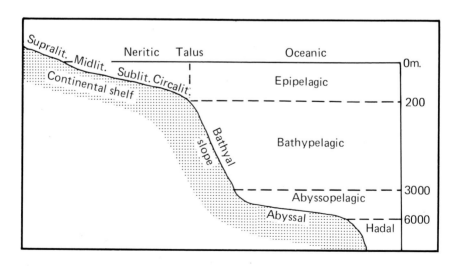

There is, of course, a constant, dynamic relationship between the seabed and the open waters, on the one hand, and the benthic species, the nekton, and the plankton, on the other, a relationship that involves considerable changes in time and space, but that follows a recognizable pattern.

Other marine zones are determined by considering the amount of solar light that penetrates to various depths (the *euphotic* zone: down to 20 to 120 meters; the *oligophotic:* down to 300 to 600 meters; and the *aphotic*, below that), or the variations in temperature (*polar, subpolar, temperate, cold*, and so on).

These are all very conventional and generalized subdivisions that are useful for compiling statistics but are only of limited value to those who are mainly interested in the collection of seashells. These people should concentrate on the continental shelf, where almost all the marine shell-bearing animals live, and especially on the neritic province, which has very different characteristics from the open sea. It occupies only about 7 per cent of the submerged area of our planet, it is not very deep, and it is exposed to the direct influence of chemical and physical factors originating on the continents (fresh-water and river sediments, the composition of the coasts, the products of human activity); its waters are relatively less transparent and less penetrable by sunlight because they are very rich in suspended mineral and vegetable substances enabling them to support an abundant and varied animal life. For these reasons, the continental shelf (or the benthoneritic environment, or the littoral system) was classified by Pérès on the basis of the distribution of the fundamental types of population found in all seas. He also introduced the concept of the *zone*, defined as "the vertical space in which the ecological conditions are constant or vary regularly between two clearly defined limits."

The seabed, which can be either *fixed* (rocks, solid organogenic deposits such as atolls, human artifacts such as jetties, dikes, posts, and so on) or *mobile* (pebbles, gravel, sand, mud, slime, detritus), is classified as follows:

The *supralittoral zone*, inhabited by organisms that must or can live out of the water all the time and that are only occasionally reached by very high tides or waves (as happens in the Mediterranean).

The *midlittoral zone*, inhabited by animals that can live either in or out of water, that is, in the sort of conditions provided by the normal ebb and flow of the tides and wave action. This zone is often subdivided into upper and lower subzones related to high and low tide levels.

The *sublittoral zone*, the upper limit of which is set by organisms that must always live under water, and the lower limit varying according to the different types of seas. It extends to the greatest depths reached by phanerogamic (seed-bearing) marine

Diagrams of sandy and rocky shores.

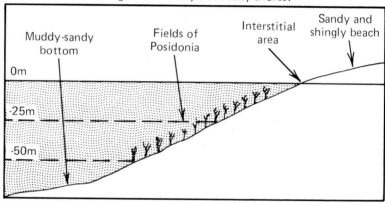

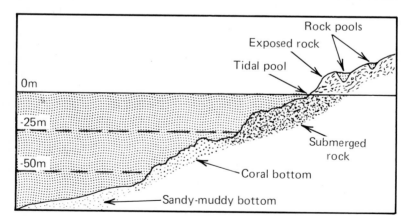

plants, such as *Posidonia* and *Zostera*, or by photophilic (light-loving) algae such as Chlorophyceae (in the Mediterranean, down to 30 or 40 meters).

The *circumlittoral zone*, reaching from the limit of the photophilic algae down to the twilight region of about 200 meters where the "shade-loving" algae live. Unless otherwise indicated, this is the zoning system used in this book.

THE MEDITERRANEAN
AND THE ATLANTIC
OCEAN, EUROPEAN
AND NORTH
AFRICAN COASTS

One might expect the Mediterranean, that cradle of civilization which was studied by Aristotle and Pliny, to be one of the most researched seas of the world. Unfortunately this is not the case. But the information obtained in the areas that have been thoroughly investigated, such as the Gulf of Naples, the Adriatic, the southern coasts of France, and a few other western sectors, is enough to support conclusions about the Mediterranean as a whole. Information about the southern and eastern parts, in particular, is still fragmentary and inadequate.[1]

It is not even possible to say for certain whether the entire Mediterranean is zoologically and geographically part of the so-called Atlantic-Mediterranean region, or whether its southeastern part, whose fauna has a large number of subtropical characteristics, should be regarded as a tropical body of water, rather than as a remnant of the primeval Tethys Sea.

On the other hand, the Strait of Gibraltar is not a biologically impassable barrier, except in certain cases (*see Fig. 12*). The Mediterranean is thus not a separate faunal entity but part of a much greater whole that encompasses the European and North African coasts of the Atlantic, in particular from the western mouth of the English Channel in the north to Cape Blanc, the Azores, Madeira,

---

[1] *Israeli scholars have, however, made a very promising start in research.*

the Canaries, and the Cape Verde Islands. It is impossible to define the boundaries clearly and to say where the populations we are considering terminate. Some species go up as far as the Kara Sea, others go down as far as the Cape of Good Hope, and still others are found on the American side of the Atlantic, all once parts of the Tethys Sea.

As has already been mentioned (*see pp. 34–35*), the marine fauna of Europe began to assume its present-day characteristics in the Miocene and Pliocene periods. The tropical species withdrew and their place was taken by migrants from the north. The animals driven out of the Mediterranean took refuge around northwestern Africa, where some still survive. But because the climate was much colder then than it is today, many of them could not adapt and have come down to us only as fossils.

Thus, of the shelled animals, 68 per cent of the Mediterranean species are also found in Scandinavian waters, and 45 per cent in the Atlantic-African region as far as Cape Verde. But such information is constantly changing as new discoveries are made, or certain conditions alter. Migrants from the Atlantic, however, seem to reach an almost impassable barrier at Sicily, which can conveniently be considered as the midpoint between the western and the eastern Mediterranean: *Mesalia opalina* (*see Fig. 97*) and *Propilidium ancyloide* have not been found beyond this point, and *Patella safiana* stops at the threshold of Gibraltar. The fauna of the eastern Mediterranean, as we shall see, is very similar to that of Japan.

Gibraltar: Passageway and Barrier

The Mediterranean and the Atlantic are joined and separated by the ridge of Gibraltar, which rises suddenly out of the strait to a depth of only 320 meters. This is one of the main reasons for both the considerable similarities and the differences between the Atlantic and Mediterranean faunas. But it is not only these 320 meters that are important: for most of the year a deep current with a speed of 2 meters per second flows from Gibraltar into the Atlantic. It is most powerful at a depth of 200 to 300 meters, but above this level, in the first 100 meters, water runs in the opposite direction, from the Atlantic to the Mediterranean. However, the higher temperature and greater salinity of the Mediterranean waters make them unsuitable for many Atlantic species that ordinarily live at such levels. Thus the interchange of faunas is not as great as the underwater topographical conditions would suggest.

The illustrations that follow have been arranged environmentally, i.e., according to habitat, and were chosen to convey an impression of the whole region on the basis of what can be collected there.

II

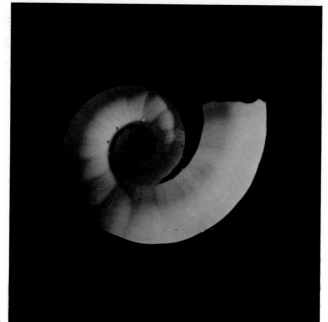

I2

11. *Bistolida stolida erythraeensis* (Sowerby), a "mysterious" intruder: typical of the Red Sea and the Gulf of Aden in shallow water under flat stones; other subspecies are widely distributed in the Indo-Pacific. This specimen was discovered on the beach at Vasto in the Abruzzi, Italy, in July 1973, and was probably brought there, unintentionally, by a human agent (×7).

12. *Spirula spirula* (L.), cosmopolitan and common in the tropical and subtropical zones of all oceans, pelagic with young at 1750–1000 m and adults at 600–200–(100) m; live specimens do not, however, manage to cross the ridge of Gibraltar (*see p. 44*); empty shells are sometimes found near Málaga and Morocco (×2⅕).

On the Rocks

13. *Patella caerulea* L., in the Mediterranean as far as the Black Sea and the Atlantic from Portugal to the Canary Islands, Madeira, the Azores; abundant in rocky midlittoral zone and on wooden jetties (×1⅓).

13

14

14. *Patella (Patellastra) ferruginea* Gmelin, in the Mediterranean, particularly Egypt, the islands, and Spain; not common, in rocky midlittoral zone beaten by waves (×2).

15

15. *Diodora italica* (Defrance), throughout the Mediterranean and in the Red Sea, though records in the latter have not been confirmed; not very common, in lower midlittoral and sublittoral zones in shallow water on rocks and stones ($\times 2\frac{1}{5}$).

16

17

50

16–17. *Haliotis (Euhaliotis) tuberculata* L., in the Mediterranean and the Atlantic from the Channel Islands→the Canary Islands, the Azores→Senegal; common in rocky midlittoral zone with algae (×1⅓ and ×½).

18. *Spondylus gaederopus* L., in the Mediterranean and the Atlantic from Portugal→Madeira→Senegal→the Cape Verde Islands; fairly common in sublittoral zone, attached to rocks (×1).

18

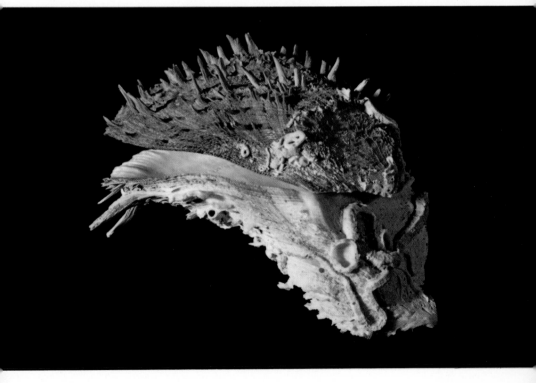

19

19. *Ostrea edulis edulis* L., in the Mediterranean→the Black Sea
and the Atlantic from the Scandinavian seas to Spain; abundant
in sublittoral zone to 80 m, in colonies attached to rock (×1).

20

20. *Lithophaga lithophaga* (L.), in the Red Sea, the
Mediterranean, and the Atlantic off Portugal; fairly common in
sublittoral zone to 100 m in holes it digs in solid rock ($\times 1\frac{2}{3}$).

Rocky Surroundings

ON THE FOLLOWING PAGE:

21. *Littorina obtusata* (L.), rather rare in the western
Mediterranean, fairly common in the Atlantic from Norway to
Gibraltar and on the American side from Labrador to Cape May,
N.J.; in sublittoral zone on rocky, stony beaches, on *Fucus*
rockweed algae, at 3 m and also dredged up at 40 m ($\times 2$).

22. *Bittium reticulatum latreillei* (Payraudeau), in the
Mediterranean, the Atlantic, all the European seas, and the
Canaries and the Azores; not common, in rock crevices and under
stones, on *Zostera* eelgrass, in lower midlittoral zone at 8–14 m,
rare on sand ($\times 3\frac{1}{2}$).

21

22

54

23. *Erosaria* (*Ravitrona*) *spurca* (L.), in the Mediterranean and the Atlantic from Portugal→St. Helena and, on the American side, the subspecies -*acicularis* Gmelin, from North Carolina→ Yucatán and Brazil and in the Antilles, Bermuda, the Bahamas; not common, in rock crevices and under stones (×4).

24

24-25. *Thais* (*Stramonita*) *haemastoma* (L.), in the Mediterranean and the Atlantic from the English Channel→the Cape Verde Islands and, on the American side, the subspecies -*floridana* (Conrad) from North Carolina→Florida and the Caribbean→Brazil, and -*canaliculata* (Gray) from northwest Florida to Texas, and on the other side of the Isthmus of Panama -*biserialis* (Blainville) from Baja California to Chile; common in rocky sublittoral zone with vegetation (×1 and ×1⅓).

25

26

26. *Pholas dactylus* L., in the Mediterranean→the Black Sea and
the Atlantic from the Lofoten Islands→southern England→the
Canaries→Morocco; fairly common in lower midlittoral zone
and just below in holes that it digs in submerged trees and in
schist, slate, limestone, and sandstone rocks (×1⅕).

27

27. *Zonaria pyrum pyrum* (Gmelin), in the Mediterranean and the Atlantic from the Canaries, Madeira→Senegal, and farther south the subspecies *-angolensis* Odhner; fairly common in rocky sublittoral zone and under stones at 10–40 m (×2).

28. *Trivia europaea* (Montagu), in the
Mediterranean and the Atlantic from
Gibraltar to southern Scotland; common in
sublittoral zone to 100 m and also in rocky
ravines and under stones ($\times 5$).

29. *Calliostoma conulum* (L.), in the
Mediterranean as far as the Black Sea and into
the Atlantic to the Canaries, Madeira, the
Azores; common in sublittoral and
circumlittoral zones to 300 m on rocks with
vegetation ($\times 5$).

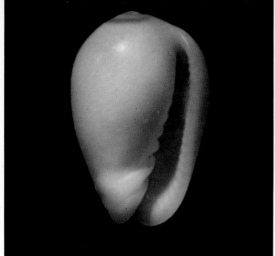

30

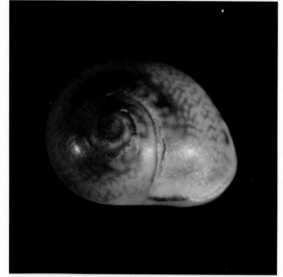

31

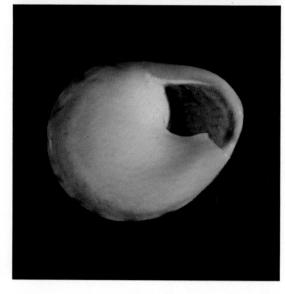

32

30. *Gibberula miliaria* (L.), in the Mediterranean and the Gulf of Suez, and in the Atlantic from Portugal to the Canaries and Madeira; common in shallow, stagnant water on algae ($\times 10$).

31–32. *Cyclope neritea* (L.), in the Mediterranean; common in sandy, muddy sublittoral zone, also in brackish water ($\times 5\frac{1}{2}$).

33. *Ensis siliqua* (L.), in the Mediterranean and the North Atlantic polar region from the Lofoten Islands→the British Isles →Morocco; common in midlittoral and sublittoral zones from 0 to 22 m, always on fine sand ($\times \frac{1}{5}$).

33

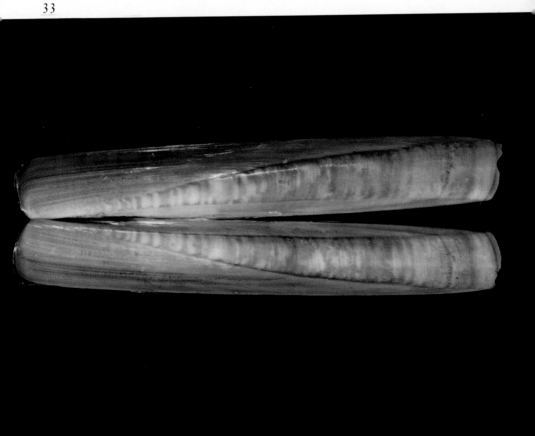

34

34. *Venerupis* (*Amygdala*) *decussata decussata* (L.), in the
Mediterranean and the Atlantic from the Lofoten Islands→
Portugal→the Canaries→Mauritania; abundant in sandy
sublittoral zone from 5 m (×3).

35

35. *Venerupis* (*Polititapes*) *aurea* (Gmelin) var. *partita* Bucquoy
and Dollfuss and Dautzenberg, of the Adriatic and the Channel
Islands; the species is found in the Mediterranean→the Black Sea
and in the Atlantic from the North Sea→Norway→Morocco→
Ghana; common in sandy sublittoral zone (×4).

36

36–37. *Gourmya* (*Thericium*) *vulgata* (Bruguière), in the Mediterranean; abundant in muddy or sandy sublittoral zone ($\times 1$ and $\times 1\frac{1}{2}$).

37

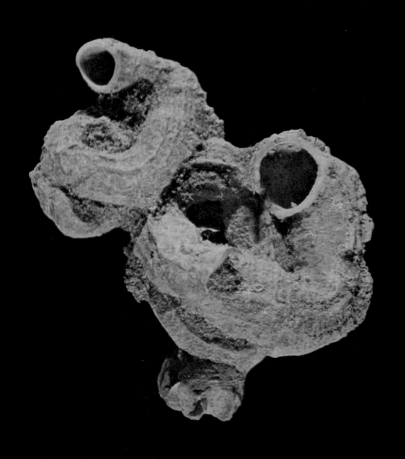

38. *Bivonia triquetra* (Bivona), in the Mediterranean and the Atlantic from Gibraltar to Portugal; common in sublittoral zone, on muddy submerged rocks as well as on other shell-bearers (×4).

39. *Venericardia* (*Cardites*) *antiquata antiquata* (L.), in the Mediterranean and the Atlantic from Gibraltar to Portugal; common in midlittoral and sublittoral zones from 0 to 30 m in coarse sand (×1½).

39

40

40. *Dentalium* (*Antalis*) *vulgare* (da Costa), in the
Mediterranean; common in sandy or muddy sublittoral zone
from 1 to 50 m ($\times$1).

41. *Lunatia catena* (da Costa), in the Mediterranean and
throughout the eastern Atlantic; common in sandy or
muddy sublittoral zone from 0 to 215 m ($\times$2).

70

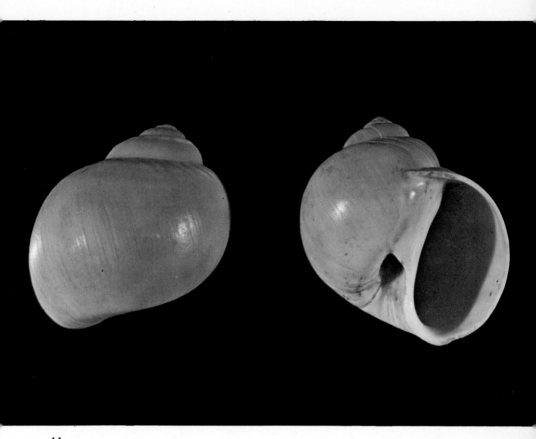

41

Shingle and Rocky, Stony Environments

ON THE FOLLOWING PAGE:

42. *Pinna nobilis* L., in the Mediterranean; common in sublittoral zone from 3 m to much deeper, fixed to the bottom among rocks and shingle (×¼).

43. *Amyclina corniculum* (Olivi), in the Mediterranean and the Atlantic from Gibraltar to Portugal; common in stony sublittoral zone in still water (×4).

44. *Pisania striata* (Gmelin), in the Mediterranean and the Atlantic from Gibraltar→the Azores; abundant in stony sublittoral zone covered with algae (×2⅓).

45. *Ocinebrina edwardsi helleriana* Brusina, in the Mediterranean, particularly Dalmatia and Sicily, and in the Atlantic from the Bay of Biscay →the Canaries and Madeira; common on stony bottoms with sand (×4).

ON THE FOLLOWING PAGE:

46. *Tricolia pulla* (L.), in the Mediterranean and the Atlantic from the North Sea→Ireland→ Portugal→the Canaries and the Azores; common from the lower midlittoral zone to 35 m on stony bottoms with algae (×7).

47. *Gourmya* (*Thericium*) *rupestris* (Risso), in the Mediterranean and the Atlantic from the mouth of the Loire to the Canaries; common in stony, steep sublittoral zone (×3).

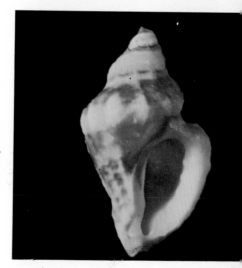

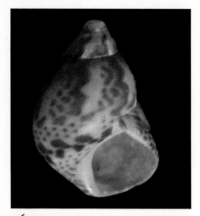

46

47

48

48. *Luria lurida* (L.), in the Mediterranean and the Atlantic from the islands at the mouth of the Tagus River→the Gulf of Guinea→ the Ascension Islands→St. Helena (unconfirmed sightings in the Antilles); common in stony, shingly sublittoral zone around 10 m and much deeper (×4).

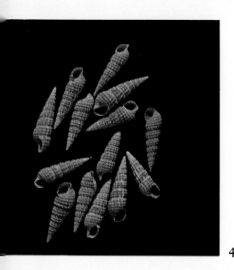 

49   50

49. *Bittium reticulatum reticulatum* (da Costa), in all the European seas, the Canaries, and the Azores; common locally on steep, stony beaches with *Zostera* eelgrass and *Codium* algae, and occasionally dredged up from much greater depths (×1).

50. *Gibbula maga* (L.), in the Mediterranean and the Atlantic from southern England→the Azores; common in sublittoral zone and beyond on muddy shingle and detritus, but also in the shallows, on algae (×1⅐).

51. *Barbatia barbata* (L.), in the Mediterranean and the Atlantic from southern Portugal→the Cape Verde Islands, but related cosmopolitan species in all the seas; common in sublittoral and circumlittoral zones on stony bottoms with algae from 4 to 480 m (×1½).

52

52. *Circomphalus casinus casinus* (L.), a subspecies typical of the Mediterranean; other subspecies are found in the Atlantic from the Scandinavian seas→ the Canaries→Senegal→Benin; common from the sublittoral zone to the seabed, from 12 to 823 m, on shingle (×1½).

53

53. *Tetrarca tetragona* (Poli), in the Mediterranean and the Atlantic from southern Norway→the Cape Verde Islands; common from the sublittoral zone to the seabed, from 5 to 2,664 m, on stony bottoms and detritus (×⅘).

The Coralline Zone

This refers to the kind of sublittoral bottom formed from the deposits of organisms, such as calcareous algae, corals, and tube worms, that produce calcium carbonate; from 15 to 25 m and below, near rocky coasts, and also on rocky bottoms in the open sea.

54–55. *Venus verrucosa verrucosa* L., in the Mediterranean and the Atlantic from Ireland→Madeira, the Canaries→ Senegal and the Cape Verde Islands; common in sand near rocks and in coralline zone (×2 and ×1).

54

56. *Coralliophila* (*Hirtomurex*) *lamellosa* (Philippi), in the Mediterranean and the Atlantic from Gibraltar to Portugal; fairly rare, in coralline zone (×7).

57. *Mantellum hians* (Gmelin), in the Mediterranean and the Atlantic from northern Norway→the Azores and the Canaries and, on the American side, in the Antilles, Bermuda, the Bahamas; fairly common among algae in coralline zone (×⅘).

57

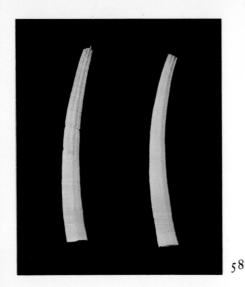

58. *Dentalium* (*Antalis*) *inaequicostatum* Dautzenberg, throughout the Mediterranean; fairly common in sublittoral and sandy or muddy circumlittoral zones from 5 to 120 m, less common in coralline zone down to 40 m (×1).

58

ON THE RIGHT AND THE FOLLOWING PAGE:

59–60. *Cymatium* (*Monoplex*) *parthenopaeum* (von Salis), in the warm waters of the western Mediterranean and in the Atlantic from Portugal→the Canaries→Guinea; it is, in fact, cosmopolitan, with forms in the American Atlantic off North Carolina→Florida→Texas→ Brazil and Bermuda, in the Pacific off the Gulf of California →Galápagos Islands, in the Indo-Pacific off Japan (especially southwest Honshu), eastern Australia→Tasmania, New Zealand, and East Africa; not common, in sandy, muddy sublittoral zone and particularly in coralline zone (the young specimen, *Fig. 59*, has the furry periostracum, which has been removed from the adult specimen on the following page) (×2 and ×1⅔).

61. *Astarte fusca* (Poli), in the Mediterranean and the Atlantic from Portugal→the Cape Verde Islands; not very common, in coralline zone (×2).

62. *Cardita* (*Glans*) *aculeata* (Poli), in the Mediterranean→ the Aegean, and in the Atlantic from Portugal→the Cape Verde Islands; in sublittoral zone from 4 to 80 m, often at the base of corals, and in the circumlittoral and bathyal zones down to 1,000 m (×2⅓).

ON THE FOLLOWING PAGES:

63. *Cymatium* (*Gutturnium*) *corrugatum* (Lamarck), in the Mediterranean and the Atlantic from the Bay of Biscay→ Portugal and Gibraltar; not common, in sublittoral, particularly coralline, zone and in sandy or muddy circumlittoral zone from 5 to 200 m (×1½).

64. *Scaphander lignarius* (L.), in the Mediterranean and the Atlantic from Norway→Gibraltar; common in shallow coralline zone in the north, deeper in the south; feeds on scaphopods (*see p. 13*) (×2).

63

89

67

ON THE PREVIOUS PAGES:

65. *Fusinus (Gracilipurpura) rostratus* (Olivi), in the Mediterranean and the Atlantic→the Canaries; common in sublittoral zone from 35 m in coral zone and in circumlittoral zone down to 180 m (×3⅓).

66. *Aporrhais serresiana* (Michaud), in the Mediterranean, and in the Atlantic from Norway→Shetland Islands→Isle of Arran (Scotland)→southwest Ireland; not very common, in coralline zone from 75 m and in circumlittoral and bathyal zones on mud down to 2,300 m (×4).

67. *Mühlfeldtia (Megerlia) truncata* (L.), a brachiopod found in the Mediterranean in coralline zone with *Gorgonia* from 30 to 50 m and below; you can see the lophophore (*see p. 17*) inside (×2½).

92

68

Sand, Mud, and Detritus

68. *Aporrhais pespelecani* (L.), in the Mediterranean and Atlantic from the Lofoten Islands→Gibraltar; common in sublittoral and sandy or muddy circumlittoral zones from 10 to 135 m (adult and young specimen, ×1¼).

69. *Hinia (Uzita) limata* (Chemnitz), in the Mediterranean and the Atlantic from the English Channel to the Canaries; common in sublittoral zone rich in organic matter ($\times 2\frac{1}{2}$).

70. *Glycymeris bimaculata* (Poli), in the Mediterranean→southern Spain and into the Atlantic→the Canaries; not common, in sandy or muddy circumlittoral zone ($\times \frac{4}{5}$).

69

70

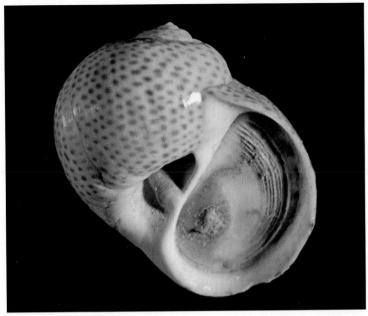

71

71. *Naticarius stercusmuscarum* (Gmelin), in the
Mediterranean and the Atlantic from Gibraltar→Portugal,
abundant in muddy and, especially, detrital sublittoral zone
($\times 2\frac{1}{3}$).

72

72. *Galeodea echinophora* (L.), in the Mediterranean; abundant in muddy-detrital sublittoral zone from 7 to 11 m, and below (×1⅓).

73. *Murex* (*Bolinus*) *brandaris* (L.), in the Mediterranean and the Atlantic from Portugal→West Africa; abundant in muddy and, especially, detrital sublittoral zone (×1½).

73

74

74–75. *Hexaplex trunculus* (L.), in the
Mediterranean and the Atlantic from Gibraltar→
Portugal→the Canaries→Morocco; abundant in
slimy and detrital sublittoral zone (×1 and ×2).

98

75

ON THE PREVIOUS PAGES AND
AT RIGHT:

76–77. *Pecten jacobaeus* (L.), in
the Mediterranean and the Atlantic
from the Canaries→the Cape Verde
Islands; common in sandy
sublittoral zone from 25 m and
among *Laminaria* oarweed, and
down to 180 m ($\times 1\frac{1}{3}$ and $\times 1$).

77

78

79
104

78. *Rudicardium tuberculatum tuberculatum* (L.), in the Mediterranean and the Atlantic from southern Britain→the Canaries and Madeira; common in sublittoral and sandy circumlittoral zones and among *Laminaria* oarweed from 15 to 100 m (×1).

79. *Neverita josephina* Risso, in the Mediterranean; common in sublittoral zone (among seaweed) on mud (×2).

80. *Callista chione* (L.), in the Mediterranean and the Atlantic from Ireland to the Canaries and the Azores; common in sublittoral and sandy circumlittoral zones down to 200 m (×1).

80

81. *Turritella communis*
Risso, in the
Mediterranean and all
European seas; abundant
in sublittoral and sandy
circumlittoral zones from
6 to 200 m and below
($\times 3\frac{1}{4}$).

82. *Archimediella*
(*Torculoidella*) *triplicata*
(Brocchi), in the
Mediterranean and the
Atlantic from Spain→the
Canaries→West Africa;
in muddy, detrital
sublittoral zone from 20
to 60 m ($\times 3\frac{1}{2}$).

ON THE FOLLOWING
PAGES:

83. *Thracia papyracea
papyracea* (Poli) in the
Mediterranean→the
Black Sea and the
Atlantic from the
Lofoten Islands→Portugal
→the Cape Verde Islands;
fairly common in muddy
and sandy-muddy
sublittoral zone (×2).

84. *Aequipecten
opercularis* (L.), in the
Mediterranean and the
Atlantic from northern
Norway→the Faroe
Islands→the Azores, the
Canaries→Spain; common
in sandy or muddy
sublittoral and
circumlittoral zones or
on other bivalves down to
200 m and below (×1).

85. *Naticarius maculatus*
(von Salis), in the
Mediterranean and the
Atlantic from Gibraltar
to Portugal; common in
sublittoral and
circumlittoral zones
down to 80 m (×2).

83

84

85

Deep Waters

86–87. *Pteria hirundo* (L.), in the Mediterranean and the
Atlantic from southern Britain→the Azores and the
Canaries; not common, in sublittoral, circumlittoral, and
bathyal zones from 5 to 1,500 m (×1).

87

88

88. *Peplum clavatum clavatum* (Poli), in the Mediterranean and the Atlantic from the Shetland Islands→the Cape Verde Islands; not common, in the sublittoral zone from 5 m, the circumlittoral around 120, and the bathyal down to 1,350 (×1).

89. *Chlamys varia* (da Costa), in the Mediterranean and the
Atlantic from Norway→the Cape Verde Islands; common in
the sublittoral zone from o to 6o m and in the bathyal down to
1,350 m (×1⅕).

90

90. *Cymatium* (*Tritoniscus*) *cutaceum* (L.), in the central-west Mediterranean and the Atlantic from the English Channel→the Canaries→the Cape Verde Islands; in sandy circumlittoral zone at 60 m and below, but also recorded at the surface, on *Haliotis* (*see Figs. 16–17*) (×1).

91. *Manupecten pesfelis* (L.), in the Mediterranean and the Atlantic from the French coast→the Cape Verde Islands; rare in the sublittoral and not very common in sandy, shingly circumlittoral zone from 10 to 225 m and even deeper (×1¼).

91

92. *Ranella olearia* (L.), in the Mediterranean and the Atlantic from southern Britain→West Africa; not common, in the circumlittoral zone and beyond; but found sporadically as far as South Africa→Australia and New Zealand (×1⅐).

93. *Corbula* (*Varicorbula*) *gibba* (Olivi), in the Mediterranean→the Black Sea and the Atlantic from the Arctic→Morocco→Angola; common in muddy, sandy midlittoral zone as far as the bathyal down to 2,200 m, and often found in the stomachs of starfish (×6½).

94

94. *Glossus humanus* (L.), in the Mediterranean and the Atlantic from Norway to the Canaries; not common, in muddy sublittoral, circumlittoral, and bathyal zones and beyond, down to 3,660 m ($\times 1\frac{1}{3}$).

95

Special Situations

95. *Haminaea hydatis* (L.), in the Mediterranean and the
Atlantic from Norway→the British Isles→Gibraltar;
common in sublittoral zone on *Laminaria* oarweed; when it
is alive only the posterior tip of the shell is visible, as the rest
is hidden by the fleshy body (×10).

96

97

96. *Mitra fusiformis zonata* Marryatt, in the Mediterranean and in the Atlantic→ the Canaries (→Cape Blanc); a very rare species found in sandy and gravelly sublittoral and circumlittoral zones, where it is the largest mitride and the only one as showy as the tropical species ($\times 3$).

97. *Mesalia (Mesaliopsis) opalina* (Adams and Reeve), in the western Mediterranean and the Atlantic from Northwest Africa→ Senegal and the Cape Verde Islands (formerly recorded off Japan); on sandy bottoms in sublittoral and circumlittoral zones ($\times 2\frac{1}{3}$).

98. *Anomia ephippium* (L.), in the Mediterranean→ the Black Sea and the Atlantic from Norway→Madeira→ the Cape Verde Islands; from o to 30 m on other shell-bearers, usually bivalves (here, on the *Gourmya vulgata; see Figs. 36–37*) ($\times 2\frac{1}{2}$).

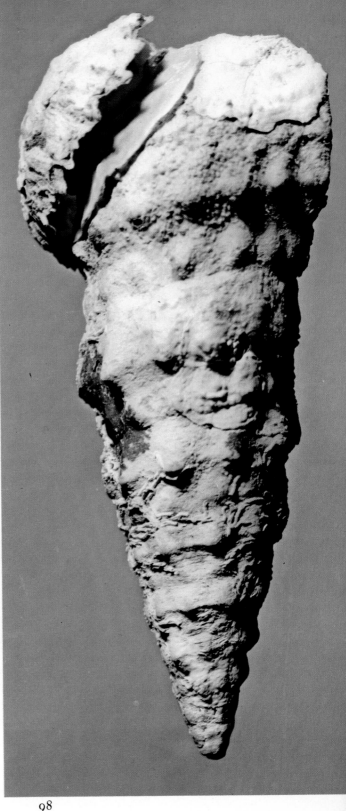

98

99

99. *Hadriania craticulata* (Brocchi), in the Mediterranean and the Atlantic from Gibraltar to Portugal; rare and usually found on banks of bivalves and echinoderms (×5).

100

100. *Cancellaria* (*Bivetiella*) *cancellata* (L.), in the West
African Atlantic from Morocco→the Cape Verde Islands and
Angola; in rocky-stony sublittoral and circumlittoral zones;
once fairly common in the Mediterranean, and still found
in its southwest, African quadrant, but rare or extinct in the
others, as a result of climatic changes (×3).

101

101. *Schilderia achatidea* (Sowerby) the rarest
cowrie of the Mediterranean. It has been found
in warmer waters, on rocky bottoms and
wooden detritus from 20 to 60 m, around Oran,
the southern coasts of Spain, and probably
southern Sicily; the young specimen shown
was discovered, empty, in the Gulf of Naples in
August 1967; in December 1975, a unique
population of 20 was found by scuba divers in
the Blue Grotto at Capri; in the Atlantic,
sporadic records along the western African
coast (Guinea) as far as Cape Fria; this species
closely resembles *Schilderia hirasei* (Roberts)
of Shikoku Island in Japan ($\times 2\frac{1}{2}$).

102

102. *Pseudosimmia carnea* (Poiret), in the
Mediterranean, especially in the west-central
area, and in the Atlantic from northwest Africa→
Madeira, the Azores, and, on the American side,
from southeast Florida→the Antilles, the
Bahamas, and Barbados; abundant around 80 m
at the base of clumps of red coral; it is not easy
to collect as it tends to drop from the coral
while being brought to the surface (×11).

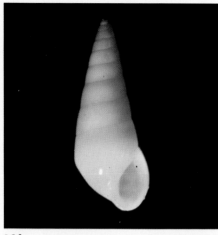

103

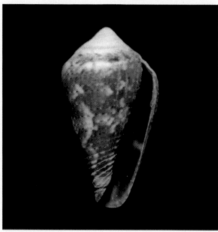
104

103. *Balcis alba* (da Costa), in the Mediterranean and the Atlantic from the Scandinavian seas to Gibraltar; a parasite of the sea urchin *Spatangus purpureus*, from 13 to 135 m ($\times 7$).

104. *Conus* (*Lautoconus*) *ventricosus* (Gmelin), in the Mediterranean, where it is the only known representative of the group, and in the Atlantic from the Bay of Biscay→the Canaries→Mauritania, Senegal→ the Cape Verde Islands; common in stony sublittoral zone with algae and under stones. It has also been recorded in the Red Sea. The wide range of its variability is responsible for over 190 nomenclatural variants ($\times 1$).

105. *Capulus hungaricus* (L.), in the Mediterranean and all European seas and the American Atlantic from Greenland→ Florida→Bermuda; a parasite of bivalves, especially *Aequipecten opercularis* (*see Fig. 84*), whose pallial cavity it pierces with its nonretractable proboscis to suck up the juice inside; also found on *Turritella* (*see Fig. 81*) and on rocks with bivalves cemented to them; a fairly rare species found from 15 to 450 m ($\times 5$).

105

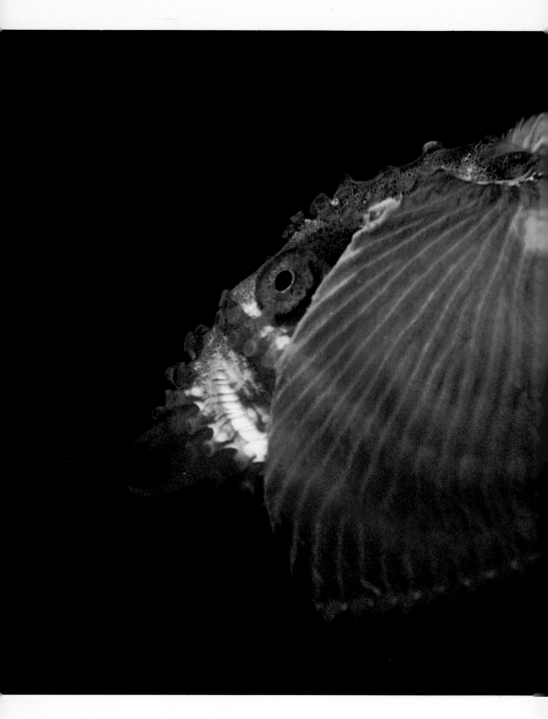

106

106. *Argonauta argo* L. ♀, a pelagic species found in the Mediterranean and all the seas of the temperate zone; only the female has a shell *(see p. 14)*, which is similar to but not the same as that of other mollusks (×1).

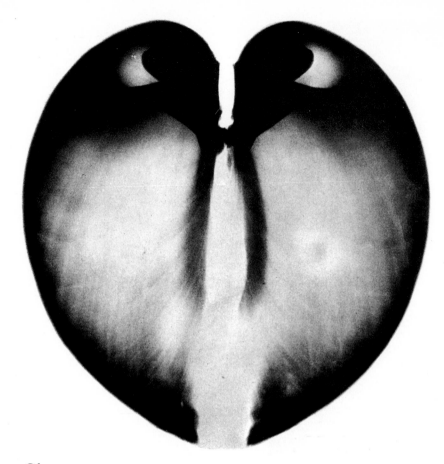

Glossus.

THE ATLANTIC OCEAN, AFRICAN COASTS

Apart from the many Mediterranean and European species that generally extend down the Atlantic coast of Africa or originate somewhere along it (various examples of which have already been given), the following species are interesting in that they are more exclusively characteristic of the African Atlantic coastline. On the whole, the fauna of this region has not been well studied; records are poor in comparison with those of analogous temperate and tropical waters because of the prevalence of sandy bottoms, which do not allow the formation of coral reefs, and because of the exposed situation of the coastline, which offers no special barriers to the ebb and flow of the tides.

107. *Cymbium cucumis* Röding, in the Atlantic off the Senegalese coast, common half-buried in fine sand from 10 to 40 m (×1⅕).

108. *Agaronia acuminata* (Lamarck), in the Atlantic from Ghana→Guinea as far as Gabon→the mouth of the Congo; common in sublittoral zone half-buried in fine sand at medium to shallow depths (×3).

109

109. *Cardium costatum* (L.), in the Atlantic from Morocco→
Mauritania→the Cape Verde Islands→Angola and farther south;
fairly common in circumlittoral zone with coarse sand (×⅔).

110. *Conus* (*Cleobula*) *genuanus* Hwass in Bruguière, in the
Atlantic from (the Canary Islands)→the Cape Verde Islands→
Senegal and especially Guinea→Sierra Leone; not common, in
rocky sublittoral zone from 0 to 10 m (×3½).

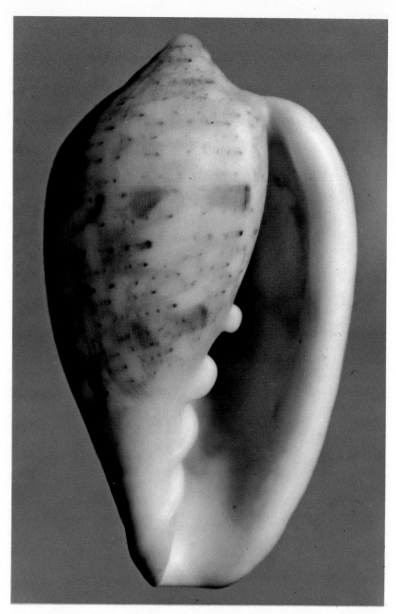

111

111. *Marginella helmatina* Rang, in the Atlantic from
Senegal→Nigeria→Gabon→Angola; common in sandy
sublittoral and circumlittoral zones ($\times 4\frac{1}{3}$).

THE ATLANTIC OCEAN, AMERICAN COASTS

Although the Isthmus of Panama might seem to be an insurmountable barrier to marine species, the two systems formed by the barrier of the American continents, the Atlantic and the Pacific, show traces, as we have already said (*see p. 35*), of a single faunistic complex.

The most characteristic element of the Atlantic side is the string of islands known as the West Indies (the Greater Antilles, the Lesser Antilles, and the Bahamas), and also Bermuda. This island entity is second only to the Indo-Malaysian archipelago in extent and contains an equally wide range of shell-bearing species.

Also noteworthy in this region is the number of correlations, or interchanges, that exist between it and the opposite coasts of Europe, the Mediterranean, and Africa.

112

112. *Nerita peloronta* L., in the Atlantic from southeast Florida→Bermuda→the Bahamas, the Antilles; abundant in rocky midlittoral zone (×2).

113. *Vermicularia spirata* (Philippi), in the Atlantic from southeast Florida→ the West Indies→Bermuda; common in shallow water associated with sponge beds and coral (×2).

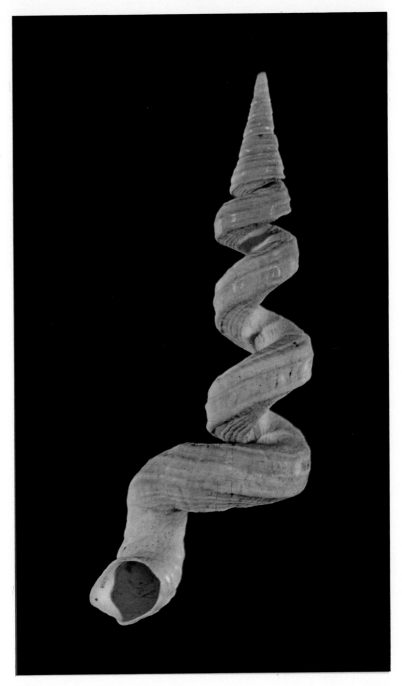

113

114

114. *Conus (Stephanoconus) regius* Gmelin, in the
Atlantic from west Florida→the Gulf of Mexico→the
Antilles, the Bahamas→Brazil; common in stony sublittoral
zone (×2½).

115. *Terebra (Myurella)* *floridana stegeri* Abbott, in the Gulf of Mexico off the Yucatán peninsula; the species extends from the coast of South Carolina to south Florida and Brazil; not common, in sandy, muddy sublittoral zone at 12 m (×2).

116

116. *Distorsio* (*Rhysema*) *clathrata* (Lamarck), in the
Atlantic from North Carolina→Florida→the Gulf of
Mexico→the Caribbean Sea, Brazil; fairly common on stony
bottoms (dredged up) from 10 to 130 m; it is very close to
D. constricta macgintyi Emerson and Puffer, of the same
area, and to *D. constricta constricta* (Broderip) and
D. decussata (Valenciennes), on the American coasts of the
Pacific from the Gulf of California to Ecuador (×1).

117. *Turbinella angulata* (Lightfoot), in the Atlantic from
Yucatán→Panama→Cuba→the Bahamas and Bermuda; fairly
common in shallow water (×⅘).

119

118. *Busycon* (*Sinistrofulgur*) *contrarium* Conrad, in the
Atlantic from New Jersey→South Carolina→Florida→the
northern Gulf of Mexico; common in sublittoral zone, where
in hunts other mollusks; it is normally sinistral (*see p. 9*)
(×⅚).

119. *Ficus communis* Röding, in the Atlantic from North
Carolina→the Bahamas→the Gulf of Mexico; abundant in
the circumlittoral zone from 20 to 200 m (×1¼).

120. *Phyllonotus pomum* (Gmelin), deep-water form, in the Atlantic from North Carolina→Florida→the Bahamas, Bermuda, the Antilles→Brazil; not common, in sublittoral zone; it hybridizes with the southern Caribbean *P. margaritensis* Abbott (×2).

121. *Charonia tritonis variegata* (Lamarck), in the American Atlantic from southeast Florida→the Bahamas, Bermuda, the Antilles, Brazil; in sublittoral zone from 10 down to 60 m; it also occurs in the eastern Atlantic among the Cape Verde Islands and St. Helena; akin to two other subspecies, *C. tritonis seguenzae* (Aradas and Benoit) of the southeast Mediterranean as far as the Aegean and *C. tritonis tritonis* (L.) of the Indo-Pacific from East Africa→the southern Pacific islands→northern and eastern Australia. These are typical fauna of the Tethys Sea heritage (*see p. 29*) (×⅓).

122. *Strombus* (*Tricornis*) *gigas* L., in the Atlantic from southeast Florida→the Bahamas, the Antilles→Bermuda; common in sandy sublittoral zone, usually among *Thalassia* eelgrass, but often gathers in herds on rocks; it is becoming scarce because it has been overexploited by the souvenir industry (×½).

148

122

123

123. Some young specimens of the previous species ($\times\frac{1}{2}$).

124. *Strombus pugilis* L., in the Atlantic from southeast Florida
to the Bahamas, the Antilles→Brazil; common on sandy and grassy
bottoms of sublittoral zone ($\times 2$).

124

125. *Strombus (Tricornis) gallus* L., in the Atlantic, rare in
southeast Florida, not common in the Bahamas, the Antilles→
Bermuda, fairly common off Jamaica→Brazil; in sublittoral
zone from 6 to 10 m ($\times \frac{5}{6}$).

126

126. *Voluta ebraea* L., in the Atlantic, typical of north and northeast Brazil; fairly common in the sublittoral zone from 20 to 40 m on coarse sand and rocks, and among corals (×1⅓).

127

127. *Voluta musica* L. form *carneolata* Lamarck ♂, typical of Barbados; the species of the southwest Caribbean is found from Haiti→Venezuela to Surinam; common in sandy sublittoral zone from 0 to 10 m and just beyond (×2).

128. *Scaphella junonia* (Lamarck), in the Atlantic from North Carolina→Florida→Texas→the Gulf of Mexico→the Yucatán Channel→Mexico; not rare but very sought after, in sublittoral and circumlittoral zones from 18 to 80 m (×2).

154

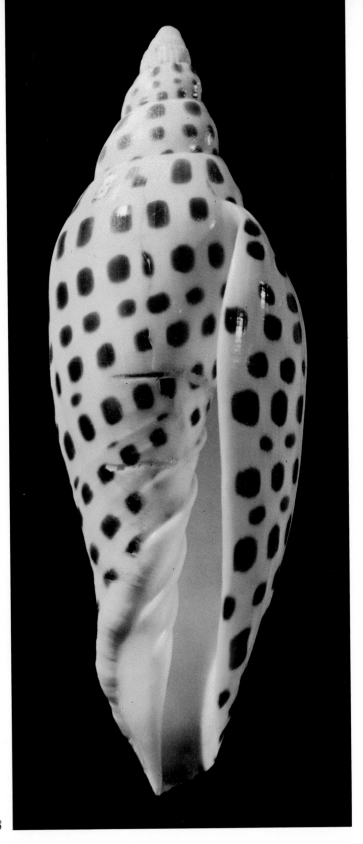

ON THE PREVIOUS PAGES:

129. *Spondylus americanus* Hermann, in the Atlantic off North Carolina→east Florida to the Bahamas, the Antilles→Brazil; frequently cemented to coral rocks from 7 to 20 m ($\times 1\frac{2}{3}$).

130

130. *Tellina radiata* L., in the Atlantic from South Carolina→ southern Florida (not very common), abundant in the Bahamas, the Antilles→Bermuda→the Guianas; in sandy sublittoral zone ($\times\frac{2}{3}$).

131. *Dinocardium robustum vanhyningi* Clench and L. C. Smith, in the Atlantic and the Gulf of Mexico, typical of west Florida from Tampa to Cape Sable; the species is found from Virginia→ north Florida→Texas→Mexico; not rare, in sublittoral and circumlittoral zones ($\times 1\frac{2}{3}$).

158

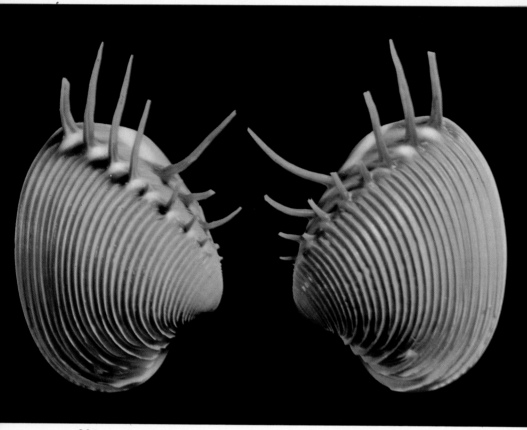

132. *Hysteroconcha dione* (L.), in the Atlantic from the Bahamas, the Antilles→Mexico→Panama; common in sandy sublittoral zone; allied with *H. lupanaria* of the American Pacific coast (*see Fig. 260*) (×2½).

133. *Lyropecten* (*Nodipecten*) *nodosus* (L.), in the Atlantic from North Carolina→Florida→Texas→the Bahamas, the Antilles, Bermuda→Brazil; recorded at Ascension Island as well; not very common, in sublittoral zone from 8 to 12 m and below, near rocky bottoms; on the other side of the Isthmus of Panama, in the American Pacific, from the Gulf of California→Peru, lives the related *L. subnodosus* (Sowerby) (×⅔).

133

ON THE FOLLOWING PAGE:

134. *Cyrtopleura* (*Scobinopholas*) *costata* (L.), in the Atlantic from Massachusetts→Florida→Texas→the Bahamas, the Antilles→ Brazil; fairly common in midlittoral and sublittoral zones on firm mud, rotten timber, and disintegrating rocks (×⅔).

135. *Anadara* (*Cunearca*) *brasiliana* (Lamarck), in the Atlantic from North Carolina→Florida→Texas→(the Bahamas and the Antilles)→Venezuela and Brazil; fairly common in sublittoral zone and below (×1).

134

135

THE INDO-PACIFIC
OCEAN

This immense oceanic area, bounded by the coasts of East Africa, southern and central-southern Asia (Tokyo), the Hawaiian Islands and Tuamotu, and northeastern and eastern Australia, contains the most abundant, homogeneous, and yet at the same time diversified, collection of fauna in the world.

There are no fewer than seven thousand species with interesting shells, the majority of which are found throughout the whole area. But there are obviously so many special conditions in such a large area, that the same basic form can appear in various guises in different zones.

Once again, the choice and criteria for grouping the species represented here reflect the objective data of biogeographical conditions and are not based upon rigid geographical principles.

Some examples of the relatively few species that are exclusive to this area.

Frontispiece: Strombus (Euprotomus) listeri T. Gray, in the Indian Ocean from the Gulf of Oman to the Bay of Bengal; dredged up from 55 to 100 m; once a legendary shell (×1).

136. *Palmadusta diluculum* (Reeve), in the Indian Ocean from East Africa (especially Aden to Durban)→Zanzibar→the Seychelles→Mauritius; not common, in coral and stony sublittoral zone; closely related to *P. ziczac* (L.), found in the same area; this species is scattered throughout the Indo-Pacific region (×4).

136

137. *Lambis (Harpago) chiragra arthritica* Röding, in the Indian
Ocean from central East Africa→northern Madagascar→Réunion→
the Seychelles→the Maldive Islands; abundant in sublittoral zone
down to 4 to 6 m on open beaches rich in algae near corals; the
typical subspecies (*see Fig. 160*) extends throughout the Pacific
(×1¼).

138. *Mauritia (Arabica) arabica immanis* Schilder and Schilder,
in the Indian Ocean from East Africa→Madagascar→the
Seychelles→Mauritius; common in sublittoral zone at 3 to 8 m in
groups on rocks and coral reefs; the other, smaller, subspecies,
M. arabica asiatica Schilder and Schilder, is found in the eastern
Indian Ocean and the Pacific, and the *M. arabica arabica* (L.)
throughout the Indo-Pacific (×1).

138

139. *Lambis truncata truncata* (Humphrey), in the Indian Ocean from central East Africa→the Bay of Bengal→the Cocos (Keeling) atolls; common on beaches to a depth of 4 to 7 m; in the Red Sea along the southern tip of the Arabian peninsula, and in the Pacific is found the other subspecies *L. truncata sebae* Kiener (this specimen has a series of supernumerary digitations: the *vexillar-fimbriate* anomaly) (×⅔).

140. *Conus (Pionoconus) magus* L., this specimen from the western range of the species, southern India; otherwise the species is common in the Pacific from the Philippines→ Melanesia→Australia (Queensland)→Great Barrier Reef; in coralline sublittoral zone (×2).

141

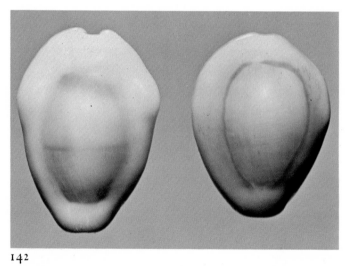

142

143

141. *Cypraea tigris* L., throughout the Indo-Pacific from East Africa→southern Japan→the southern Pacific islands as far as Hawaii→Tuamotu→New Caledonia→ eastern and northeastern Australia; very common in sublittoral zone down to 25 m; and *Cypraea (Pantherinaria) pantherina* Lightfoot, found only in the Red Sea, from Suez to Djibouti and Aden, common in same habitat. These are evidently related shells distinguished by a marked variance in the extent of their distribution (×¾).

142. *Monetaria moneta* (L.) and *Monetaria (Ornamentaria) annulus* (L.), very common throughout the whole Indo-Pacific area (the former found as far as the Galápagos Islands); in midlittoral zone half-buried in sand, on rocks, and on coral reefs, where they tend to be the only mollusks visible (×2).

143. *Mauritia (Leporicypraea) mappa* (L.)., widely distributed in the Indo-Pacific with some gaps: rare from East Africa→Mauritius→Sri Lanka, common from Indonesia→Japan (especially the Ryukyu Islands)→ the Philippines, not common from Micronesia→ Melanesia→Polynesia, rare in northern Australia; in sublittoral zone from 3 to 10 m underneath coral or lava rocks and in littoral crevices and pools (×¾).

ON THE FOLLOWING PAGES:

144. *Erronea (Adusta) onyx onyx* (L.), the species frequent in the Indo-Pacific, with some local subspecies (the specimen shown is a typical eastern subspecies), from East Africa→Indonesia→ Japan (especially central and southern Honshu)→the Philippines→ Micronesia→Melanesia as far as Fiji→northern Australia; common in sublittoral zone from 3 to 30 m (×4).

145. *Talparia talpa* (L.), throughout the Indo-Pacific from East Africa as far as the Red Sea→Indonesia→Japan (southern Honshu) →the southern Pacific islands as far as Tuamotu and Tahiti→New Caledonia→northeastern Australia; common on coral reefs from midlittoral zone to 10 m and below, but with periodic "disappearances" presumably caused by migrations toward the bottom or under sand (×2⅔).

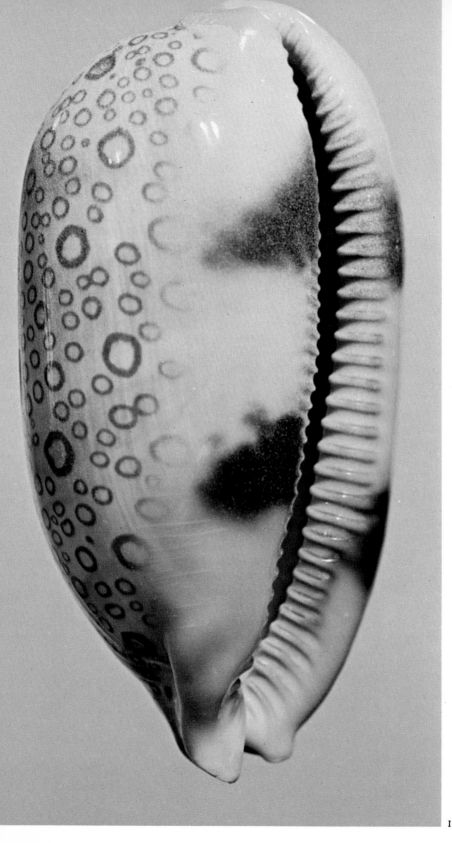

146. *Lyncina argus* (L.), widely distributed in the Indo-Pacific, but not very common and even rare, from central East Africa→ Sri Lanka→Indonesia→Japan (especially Amami)→the Philippines →the Solomon Islands→Samoa→Tonga and as far as northern and northeastern Australia; in sublittoral zone on coral rocks from 4 to 30 m and below ($\times 2\frac{1}{3}$).

147. *Mauritia mauritiana* (L.), throughout the Indo-Pacific from East Africa→Sri Lanka→Sumatra→southern Shikoku, Japan→ southern Pacific islands as far as Hawaii→Tuamotu→New Caledonia→northeastern Australia; very common in the highly oxygenated midlittoral waters of coasts beaten by surf, around 7 to 8 m ($\times \frac{5}{6}$).

148

148. *Volva volva* (L.), in the Indo-Pacific from
East Africa→southern Japan→Micronesia→
Fiji→northern and northwestern Australia;
common in sublittoral zone on madrepores from
10 to 20 m (×1⅓).

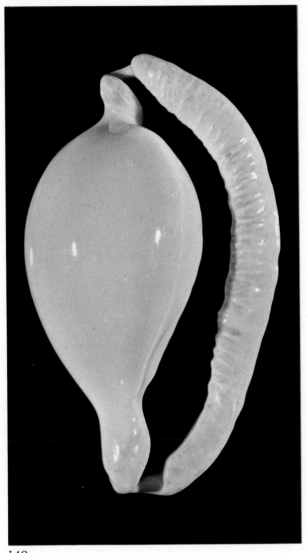

149

149. *Ovula ovum* (L.), in the Indo-Pacific from
central East Africa as far as Madagascar→
southern Japan→the southern Pacific islands as
far as the Marshall Islands→northwestern and
northeastern Australia; common in sublittoral
zone from 6 to 18 m on madrepores (×1⅘).

150   151

150. *Conus* (*Regiconus*) *aulicus* L., in the Indo-Pacific from
central East Africa→Indonesia→the Philippines→the Ryukyu
Islands→Micronesia→Melanesia→northern Australia; not common,
on coastal barrier reefs from the tidemark to 10 m (×1).

151. *Gastridium geographum* (L.), widely distributed in the
Indo-Pacific from East Africa→Indonesia→the Philippines→
southern Japan→Micronesia→Melanesia→northwestern Australia;
common in sublittoral zone on sandy detritus from the tidemark
to 10 m (×1).

152. *Conus (Cleobula) betulinus* L., widely distributed in the Indo-Pacific from East Africa as far as the Red Sea and Madagascar→the Philippines→ southern Japan→Australasia as far as northern Australia; fairly common in sandy sublittoral zone from 10 to 20 m ($\times 1\frac{3}{4}$).

153

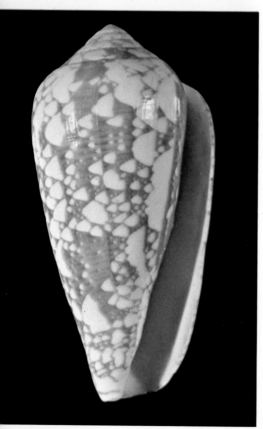

153. *Conus (Lithoconus) caracteristicus* G. Fischer, on the borderline of the Indian and Pacific oceans, from the Batan Islands, the Philippines→Sumatra; not uncommon, in muddy sublittoral zone with algae, down to 20 m ($\times 1\frac{2}{3}$).

154. *Conus (Darioconus) pennaceus* Born, in the Indo-Pacific from East Africa as far as the Red Sea→Indonesia→ Micronesia→Polynesia; fairly common in sandy sublittoral zone near rocks ($\times 1\frac{1}{2}$).

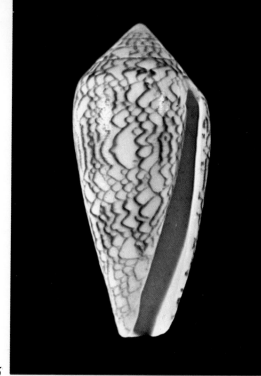

155. *Conus (Cylindrus) textilis*
L., throughout the entire Indo-
Pacific area from East Africa
(especially Natal→the Red Sea)
→Indonesia→the Philippines→
central Honshu, Japan→
Australasia as far as northeastern
Australia; very common from
the low-water mark to 8 m
(×1).

156. *Conus (Punticulis) arenatus*
Hwass in Bruguière, widely
distributed in the Indo-Pacific
from East Africa as far as the
Red Sea→Indonesia→northern
Amami, Japan→Melanesia→
northeastern Australia; common
in sublittoral zone from 10 to 20
m (×2).

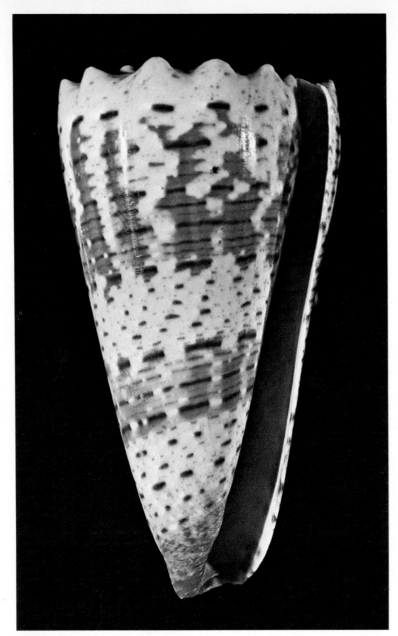

157

157. *Conus (Rhombus) imperialis* L., widely distributed in the Indo-Pacific from central East Africa→Indonesia→southern Amami, Japan→Micronesia→Polynesia→the northern Great Barrier Reef; common in sublittoral zone from 10 to 20 m ($\times 1\frac{2}{3}$).

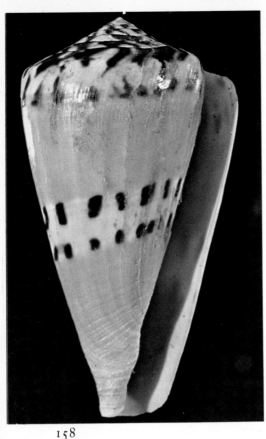

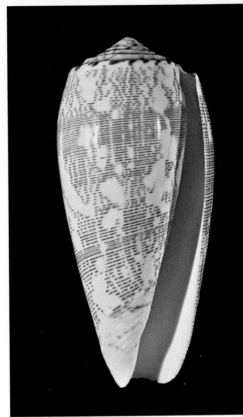

158   159

158. *Conus (Rhizoconus) mustelinus* Hwass in Bruguière, in the
Indo-Pacific from Indonesia→the Kii Peninsula, Japan→
Micronesia→northern Australia; not very common, in sandy
sublittoral zone under stones from 4 to 10 m ($\times 1\frac{1}{2}$).

159. *Conus (Strioconus) striatus* L., widely distributed in the
Indo-Pacific from East Africa→(the Red Sea)→Indonesia→
southern Ryukyu Islands, Japan→Polynesia→Micronesia→
Melanesia→north and northeastern Australia; common in coarse
sand from the tidemark to 8 m ($\times 1\frac{1}{5}$).

160. *Lambis (Harpago) chiragra chiragra*
(L.) ♀, found in the central and eastern
Indo-Pacific from Sri Lanka→Andaman
Islands→the Philippines→the Ryukyu Islands,
Japan→the Marshall Islands→Tuamotu→New
Caledonia→northern Australia→Indonesia;
fairly common on sandy and coral coasts
exposed to surf or in tidal pools from low-
water mark to 4 m; the shell shown belongs
to a female; the males are half the size and
are known as the *rugosa* (Sowerby) form,
which is not very distinguishable from the
other subspecies *L. chiragra arthritica* Röding
found only in the Indian Ocean (*see Fig. 137*)
(×⁶⁄₇).

ON THE FOLLOWING PAGES:

161. *Lambis (Millepes) digitata* (Perry) ♂,
in the Indo-Pacific from central East Africa→
Mauritius→the Philippines→Samoa; a
moderately rare species about which not
everything is known. It probably lives on
coral reefs from 2 to 6 m, but this has not
been ascertained (×1⅕).

162. *Lambis lambis* (L.) ♂, widely
distributed in the Indo-Pacific from central
East Africa→Madagascar→Mauritius,
Maldive Islands→Persian Gulf→Sri Lanka→
Andaman Islands→the Philippines→the
Ryukyu Islands, Japan→Micronesia→
Melanesia as far as Tonga and Cook Islands→
northeast and northern Australia; abundant
in herds on shallow sandy beaches or on coral
detritus associated with algae from low-water
mark to 10 m (×1).

184

161

186

163

163. *Lambis crocata crocata* (Link), widely distributed in the Indo-Pacific from central East Africa→the Andaman Islands→the Philippines→the Ryukyu Islands, Japan→the Marshall Islands→ Samoa→the New Hebrides→the Great Barrier Reef→ (unconfirmed records off the Cape York Peninsula and Cape Arnhem, Australia)→Indonesia; common on beaches exposed to surf from low-water mark to 4 m; the specimen depicted is a deviant one, morphologically lacking the third upper digitation; confined to the Marquesas Islands is the double-sized giant subspecies *L. crocata pilsbryi* Abbott ($\times 1\frac{1}{3}$).

ON THE FOLLOWING PAGES:

164. *Oliva miniacea* Röding, form *marrati* Johnson, the color variation most frequent in the Philippines, belonging to a species otherwise found in the central and eastern Indo-Pacific from Indonesia→Japan→Micronesia→Melanesia→eastern and north-eastern Australia and the Great Barrier Reef; common in sandy midlittoral and sublittoral zones from 0 to 9 m and just below ($\times 3$).

165. *Oliva annulata* Gmelin, form *intricata* Dautzenberg, a coloration of a variant species found in the Indo-Pacific from East Africa→the Philippines→Indonesia→northern Australia→ Micronesia, Fiji; common in sandy midlittoral and sublittoral zones down to 7 m ($\times 3\frac{2}{3}$).

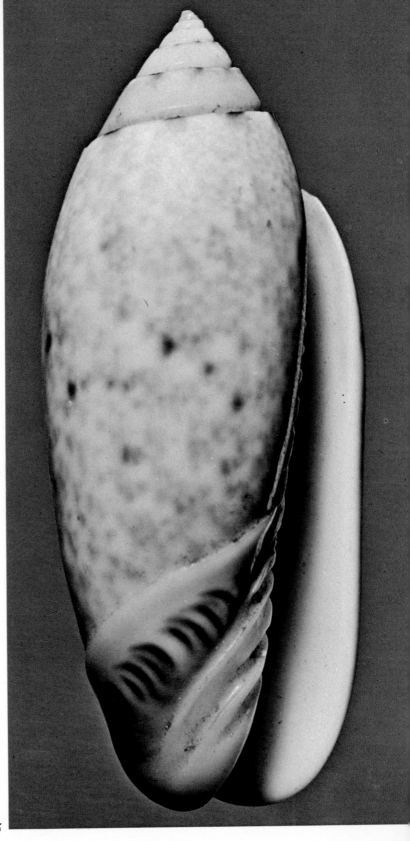

166

166. *Tridacna* (*Chametrachea*) *squamosa* Lamarck, in the
Indo-Pacific from central East Africa→the Red Sea, the
Philippines→Honshu, southern Japan→Indonesia→
Micronesia as far as Samoa and Tonga→Melanesia→northern
Australia and especially the Great Barrier Reef; common in
crevices in coral reefs below the low-water mark usually in
somewhat protected localities; in reef moats ($\times \frac{2}{3}$).

167. *Chicoreus ramosus* (L.), from East Africa (especially
the Red Sea→Natal)→the Gulf of Mannar, India→the
Philippines→southern Japan→the southern Pacific islands→
the Great Barrier Reef and north and northwestern Australia;
abundant in sublittoral zone rich in bivalves ($\times \frac{5}{6}$).

168

168. *Monodonta labio* (L.), in the
Indo-Pacific from Indochina→south
of Hokkaido, Japan→Melanesia→
northern Australia from Queensland
to northwest Australia; common in
rocky midlittoral zone, in crevices and
under stones ($\times 2\frac{1}{4}$).

169. *Cassis cornuta* (L.) ♀, widely
distributed in the Indo-Pacific from
central and northern East Africa
as far as the Red Sea→Indonesia→the
Ryukyu Islands, Japan→the
Philippines→Micronesia→Polynesia,
Hawaii→Melanesia→the Great
Barrier Reef and northeast and
northern Australia; common in herds
on sandy intertidal beaches and coral
detritus from 2 to 30 m ($\times \frac{2}{3}$).

194

170. *Tibia insulaechorab* Röding and *Tibia martinii* Marrat, examples of Indo-Pacific fauna with restricted distribution. The former (not rare) is found in the Red Sea (the *curta* Sowerby form)→the Arabian Sea as far as Malabar, between 18 to 30 m; the latter (rare), in the Philippines, on circumlittoral bottoms at depths as far as 250 m ($\times 1\frac{1}{2}$).

171. *Pinctada margaritifera* (L.), throughout the Indo-Pacific, where it is the commonest and "classic" pearl-bearing oyster, from East Africa as far as the Red Sea→southern and Southeast Asia→southern Japan→the southern Pacific islands →the Great Barrier Reef (unconfirmed records in Queensland); abundant in sublittoral zone on coarse sand and coral detritus from 0.50 to 25–40–75 m ($\times\frac{1}{3}$).

171

172. *Turbo* (*Lunatica*)
marmoratus L., widely
distributed in the Indo-Pacific
from central East Africa→the
Philippines→southern Amami,
Japan→Melanesia→Torres
Strait, Australia; common in
sublittoral zone rich in algae
from 15 to 40 m (×1⅙).

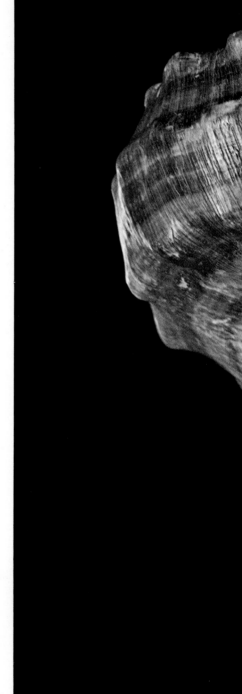

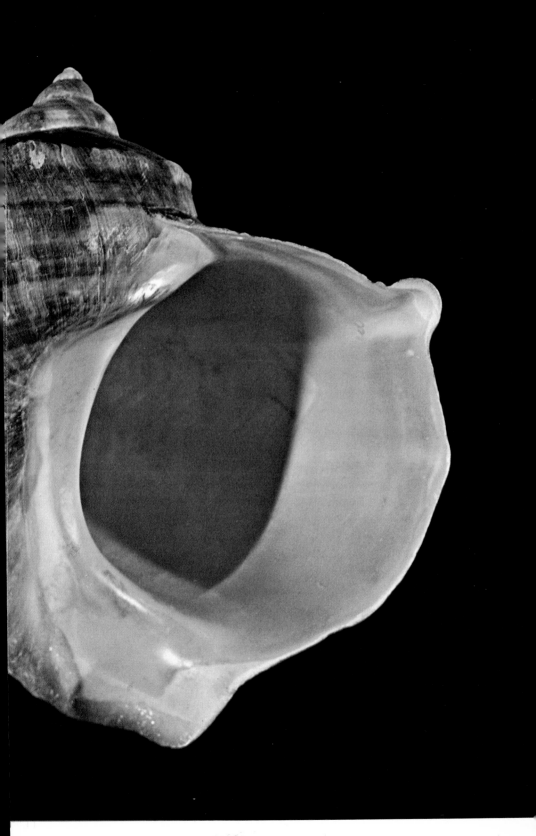

173   174

173. *Cerithium nodulosum* Bruguière, widely distributed in the
Indo-Pacific from East Africa→the Philippines→Amami, Japan
→Micronesia→northern Australia; common in sandy lower
midlittoral and sublittoral zones down to 10 m ($\times\frac{3}{4}$).

174. *Mitra stictica* (Link), in the Indo-Pacific from central East
Africa→the Philippines→the Ryukyu Islands, Japan→Micronesia→
Polynesia; common in sandy, sometimes rocky sublittoral zone
and under stones from 10 to 18 m ($\times\frac{2}{3}$).

175. *Codakia* (*Lentillaria*) *exasperata* (Reeve), in the Indo-Pacific
from East Africa→southern Japan→Melanesia (related species
are found in Australia and in the American tropical zone);
common on exposed sandy beaches from lower midlittoral zone
to 10–15 m (×2).

176

177

176. *Phalium glaucum* (L.), in the Indo-Pacific from East Africa →the Gulf of Oman→Sri Lanka→Indonesia→the Ryukyu Islands, Japan→the Philippines→Melanesia→(Torres Strait, Australia); common from midlittoral zone to 18 m on sand near dead coral. On the left side of this specimen you can see the malleated markings typical of older specimens (×⅔).

177. *Harpa major* Röding, throughout the Indo-Pacific from East Africa as far as the Red Sea→Sri Lanka→the southern Pacific islands as far as the Philippines→the Pacific coasts of Shikoku, Japan→Polynesia, as far as Hawaii and the Marquesas→northern Australia; not common, in sublittoral zone from 8 to 50 m and just below in sandy and rubbly bottoms (×¾).

178. *Argonauta hians* Lightfoot ♀, widely distributed in warm tropical seas, and common in the Indo-Pacific pelagic zone from East Africa to China, Japan, the southern Pacific islands, Australia and as far as New Zealand; it serves as an egg case (*see p. 14*) (×1).

178

179

179. *Cypraeacassis rufa* (L.), widely
distributed in the Indo-Pacific but not
continental Asia, from East Africa (especially
Durban→the Gulf of Aden)→the Maldive
Islands→Java→the southern Ryukyu Islands,
Japan→the Philippines→Melanesia and as far as
Palmyra Island→Tuamotu→Cape York,
Australia; abundant in midlittoral zone as far
down as 2 m on coralline sand rich in algae and
peopled by sea urchins. A developing genetic
division between an Indian and a Pacific form is
becoming evident ($\times \frac{2}{3}$).

180

180. *Harpa amouretta* (Röding) and *Harpa harpa* (L.), both
found in the Indo-Pacific, the former from East Africa→(the Red
Sea)→Natal→Sri Lanka→the Philippines→Shikoku, Japan→the
southern Pacific islands as far as Hawaii and the Marquesas
→northeastern Australia; common on sandy shores and under
corals between 0 and 10–20 m; the latter from the southern
Ryukyu Islands, Japan→the Philippines→Indonesia (and westward
→Somalia→Mauritius)→northern Micronesia→eastern Melanesia
→Great Barrier Reef (sporadic records); common in tidal rock
pools and in the sublittoral zone of rocky coasts from 4 to 16 m
(×1½).

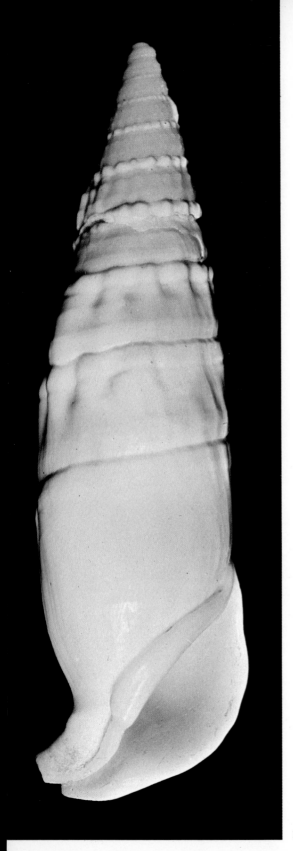

181. *Rhinoclavis vertagus*
(L.), species of a group
widely distributed in the
Indo-Pacific; it is found from
southern Japan→the southern
Pacific islands→northern
Australia; common in coral
reef lagoons from the
midlittoral zone to just below,
buried in clean sand (×3).

182. *Terebra maculata maculata* (L.), covering the whole Indo-Pacific area, found from East Africa→the Philippines→southern Japan→the southern Pacific islands→northern and western Australia and also as far as Cocos Island, Costa Rica, off the American coast; quite common everywhere on sublittoral sandy bottoms near coral reefs (×1¼).

Conus

208

JAPAN

To eighteenth-century zoologists, the many similarities in shape and structure between Mediterranean and Japanese marine fauna were a puzzle until the discovery of the past existence of the Tethys Sea clarified the matter.

This is one of the best-documented marine areas of the world. Thanks to its conspicuous north-south orientation, to its considerable submarine ridges that, like Gibraltar (*see pp. 44–45*), prevent many bathyal and bathypelagic forms from being widely distributed, and to the currents that make the difference between the summer and winter temperatures of the Japanese seas greater than in the rest of the ocean, the fauna here ranges from the tropical (in the more southern islands), to the subtropical and the temperate. The different types are amalgamated in some areas but not in others, according to the kind of conditions and convergences we have already met in the Mediterranean.

The examples that follow are a selection of both purely local species and species that are distributed throughout a much larger area.

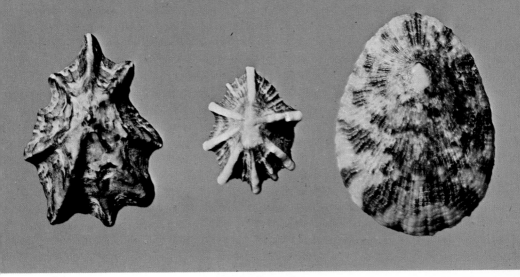

183. *Thatcheria mirabilis* Angas, on Pacific coast of central Honshu and Shikoku→Taiwan→the Philippines; not common, in circumlittoral zone from 55 to 400 m in fine sandy and muddy bottoms (×2).

184. *Patelloida* (*Collisellina*) *saccharina lanx* (Reeve), common in upper midlittoral zone; *Anthosiphonaria sirius* (Pilsbry), common in midlittoral zone; *Cellana toreuma* (Reeve), also common in midlittoral zone; all are found on rocky coasts: the first and third throughout Japan→the Marianas→the Philippines→ Hong Kong→Taiwan, the second (which is a tectibranch or "amphibious" mollusk) from Honshu→Kyushu→Okinawa→Korea (×1).

ON THE FOLLOWING PAGES:

185. *Clanculus gemmulifer* Pilsbry, in Japan from the Noto peninsula, Honshu→west coast of Kyushu; not common, in lower midlittoral zone in rock crevices and on stones (×2).

186. *Pyrene testudinaria tylerae* (Griffith and Pidgeon), in Japan from southern Honshu→Kyushu and throughout the tropical Pacific; common below the low-water mark, to 20 m, among seaweeds on rocks (×3).

187. *Spondylus barbatus* Reeve, in Japan from Honshu→Shikoku →Kyushu and southeast Asia; common cemented to holdfasts below the lower midlittoral zone, to 20 m (×1½).

185

186

187

188

189

188. *Batillus cornutus* (Lightfoot), from southern Hokkaido→ Shikoku→Kyushu and Korea; abundant on rocks (×1).

189. *Pharaonella perrieri* (Bertin), in Japan, characteristic of Honshu and Kyushu; fairly common in fine sandy midlittoral zone and down to 20 m (×1).

190. *Amusium japonicum japonicum* (Gmelin), in Japan from Honshu→Kyushu and Okinawa; common from 10 to 100 m on fine sand; related to two other subspecies: *-formosum* Habe from Taiwan and South China Sea and *-balloti* (Bernardi) from New Caledonia and northern Australia (×⅔).

190

191

192

191. *Architectonica trochlearis* (Hinds), in Japan from central Honshu→Shikoku and Kyushu→the Philippines; common in sublittoral zone from 35 to 60 m on sandy and muddy bottoms (×2).

192. *Xenophora pallidula* (Reeve), in Japan from northwest and southern Honshu→Shikoku and Kyushu→the Philippines, but widely recorded in the Indo-Pacific; common in sublittoral zone on shingle and detritus from 50 to 100 m; attaches other shells to itself as camouflage (×1⅓).

193. *Architectonica trochlearis* (Hinds) (*see Fig. 191*) and *Architectonica maxima* (Philippi), in Japan from central Honshu→ Shikoku and Kyushu, but found also as far as South Africa (Natal, Zululand), Sri Lanka, and Northern Australia; on sandy bottoms from 10 to 50 m (×1⅓).

193

194

194. *Tristichotrochus aculeatus* (Sowerby), in Japan, in central and southern Honshu→Shikoku→Kyushu; not common, in sublittoral and circumlittoral sandy bottoms at 20 to 200 m (×7).

195

195. *Ginebis argenteonitens hirasei* Taki and Otuka, in Japan, from northeast of the Miura peninsula→Kashima Nada; not common, in circumlittoral fine sandy bottoms at 50 to 400 m; it is naturally of mother-of-pearl only ($\times 2\frac{1}{3}$).

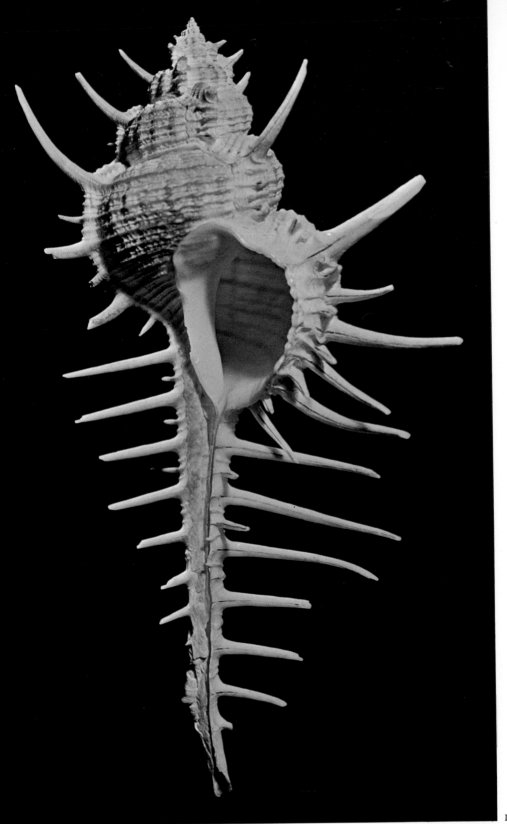

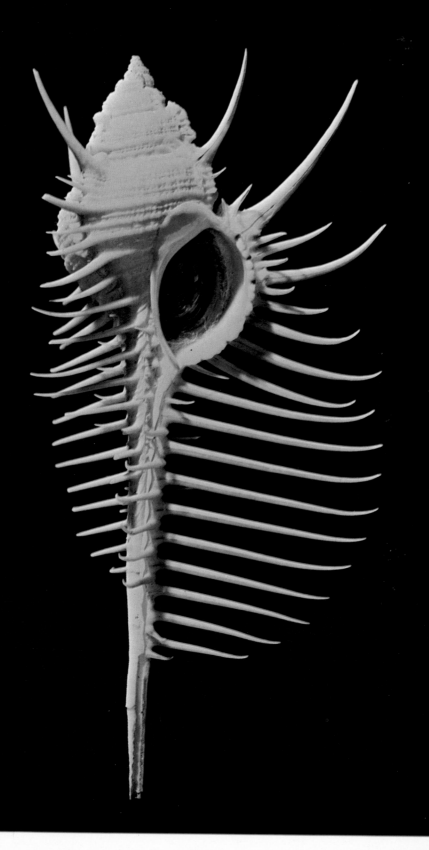

196. *Murex troscheli* Lischke, in Japan from central and southern Honshu→Shikoku and Kyushu, and→Taiwan→East China Sea; in sublittoral zone from 10 to 50 m (×1⅓).

197. *Murex pecten* Lightfoot, in Japan from central Honshu →Kyushu and the Philippines→Indonesia (as far as Malabar, recorded also in East Africa) and farther south in the western Pacific (as far as eastern Australia); in circumlittoral zone from 35 to 60 m (×1¼).

198

198. *Latiaxis* (*Tolema*) *japonicus* (Dunker), in Japan from central Honshu→Shikoku→Kyushu→Okinawa and Taiwan→South China Sea; common in circumlittoral sandy bottoms from 30 to 200 m (×2).

199. *Guildfordia yoka* (Jousseaume), in central and southern Japan; not common, in circumlittoral zone from 200 to 250 m (×1).

199

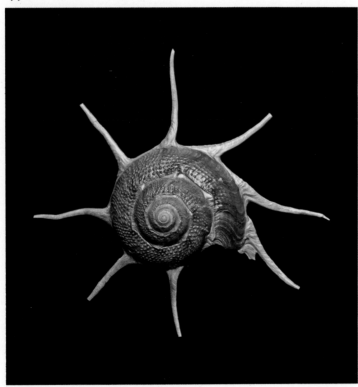

200. *Mikadotrochus hirasei*
(Pilsbry), in Japan on the
southwest Pacific coast;
fairly rare, in circumlittoral
and bathyal zones from 125 to
180 m and below ($\times 1\frac{1}{3}$).

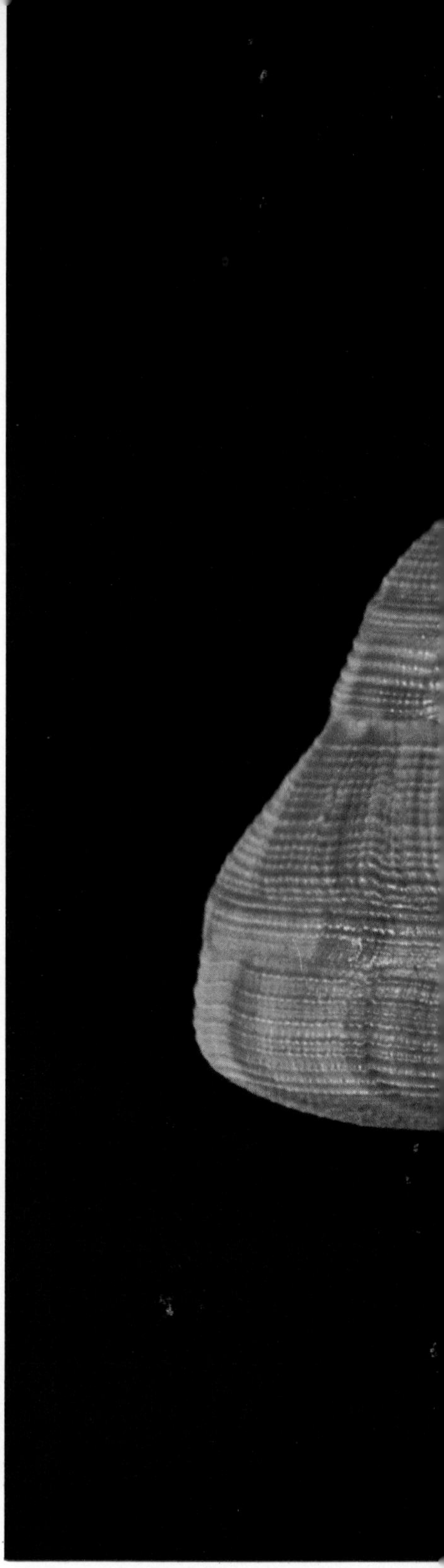

Thatcheria

226

∧

THE INDO-PACIFIC OCEAN

The Indo-Malaysian Archipelago and Related Areas

This is the largest archipelago in the world, and it is linked together by seas with wide zones not more than 200 meters deep, which are part of the neritic province (*see p. 37*) and very favorable to the circulation of life. No other area in the world approaches the Indo-Malaysian archipelago in the richness of species and characteristic shell forms, some of which are purely local, while many others have their center of distribution here and extend from north to south. The greater the distance from this focal point, the fewer varieties of fauna there are, and the new communities one does encounter do not begin to compensate for those left behind. When one goes beyond Tonga, Fiji, the Solomon Islands, and the Bismarck Archipelago, the action of the great oceanic currents, the majority of which flow from east to west, drastically limits possibilities for the further continuous distribution of shell-bearing animals.

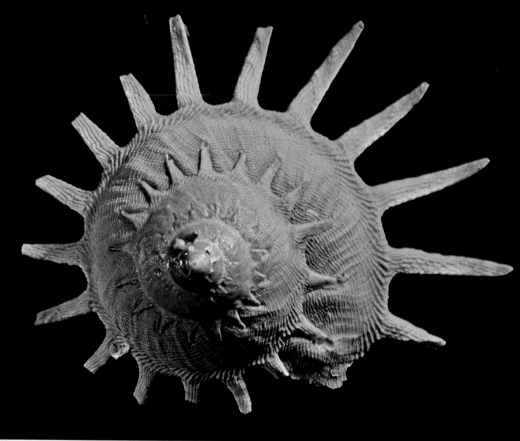

201

201. *Xenophora* (*Haliphoebus*) *solaris* (L.), typical of the Philippines and the Sulu Archipelago→Celebes→Halmahera, Moluccas; rather rare, in deep, muddy sublittoral zone (×1⅖).

202. *Chicoreus palmarosae* (Lamarck), in the central Indo-Pacific, mainly around the islands, from Sri Lanka, especially, and the Malaysian archipelago→the Moluccas→Mindanao→northwest New Guinea; not common, in shallow, rocky sublittoral zone from 6 to 20 m, but sometimes down to 45 m (×1⅖).

203

203. *Epitonium scalare* (L.), in the Pacific islands from
Honshu, Japan→Taiwan→southern China→Hainan→the
Philippines→the Moluccas→New Guinea→Fiji→
northeastern Australia; not very rare, in circumlittoral zone
with coral detritus from 36 to 60 m; this is an aged specimen
($\times 1\frac{4}{5}$).

204

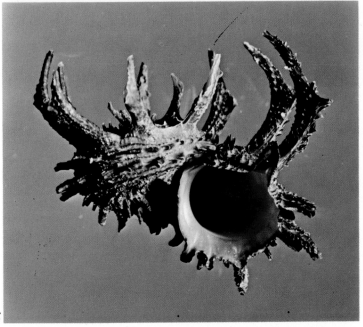

205

206

ON THE PREVIOUS PAGE:

204. *Haliotis asinina* L., in the Pacific islands from southern Japan→the Philippines→eastern Indonesia→New Guinea→ the Great Barrier Reef, northern Australia (recorded also on Inhaca Island, off Mozambique); common in lower' midlittoral zone and just below on rocky coasts (×1).

205. *Angaria delphinus* (L.) form *melanacantha* Reeve, typical of the Philippines and closely related zones; the species is not common, on coral reefs throughout the western Pacific from Japan to Fiji (×1½).

207

206. *Nautilus macromphalus* Sowerby, a local species found in
New Caledonia and the Loyalty Islands; rare, mainly in the
benthic circumlittoral and bathyal zones and in the nektonic
epipelagic and bathypelagic as well (×⅘).

207. *Nautilus scrobiculatus* Lightfoot, found off eastern New
Guinea→the Bismarck and Solomon archipelagoes; extremely
rare, probably found in the benthic bathyal and nektonic
bathypelagic zones; but no complete biological survey has been
carried out (×⅘).

208. *Nautilus pompilius* L., in the Pacific islands from the Ryukyu Islands, Japan→the Philippines→Micronesia and as far as Fiji, but the real area of distribution might be more limited because, instead of sinking to the bottom, the shells of dead specimens float on the surface and in midwater and are carried by the currents, thus achieving a spurious and much wider distribution; common in nektonic epipelagic and bathypelagic zones from 50 to 650 m, but in a strict sense in the benthic circumlittoral and bathyal zones, swimming just above the bottom in order to feed on crabs and carrion (×¾).

209. *Hippopus hippopus* (L.), in the islands of the Indo-Pacific from Sumatra→the Philippines→the Ryukyu Islands, Japan→Micronesia→Melanesia→northern Australia and as far as Tonga; on sandy bottoms among coral reefs down to 7 m (×1).

210

211

236

210. *Lioconcha ornata* (Dillwyn) and *Lioconcha fastigiata* (Sowerby), both in the Pacific islands from southern Japan→Micronesia →Melanesia→northwestern Australia; the former not very common, on sandy coastal bottoms; the latter fairly common in deeper coral and sand (×1).

211. *Fragum unedo* (L.), belonging to a genus widely distributed in the Indo-Pacific. This species is found from Amami, Japan→Micronesia →Melanesia and as far as northeastern Australia; common in coral-sandy lower midlittoral zone and just below (×1⅔).

212. *Lopha cristagalli* (Sowerby), in the Indo-Pacific islands from the Coromandel Coast→Indonesia→Amami, Japan→the Marianas →the Caroline Islands→southern New Guinea→ Queensland, Australia; fairly rare, below the low-water mark, usually fixed to coral (×⅔).

212

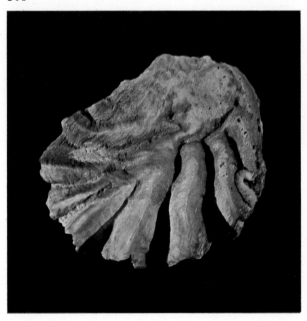

237

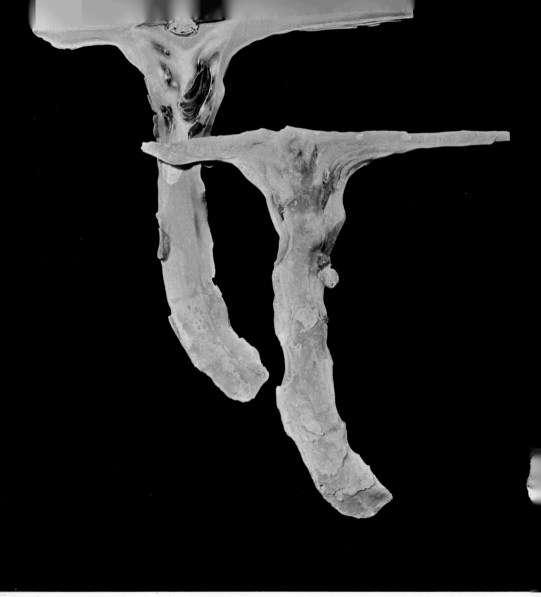

213

213. *Malleus albus* Lamarck, in the Pacific islands, mainly in the south, from northeastern Australia→east-central New Guinea→ the Solomon Islands, the Bismarck Archipelago, and then with increasing rarity→the Caroline Islands→the Marianas→southern Honshu, Japan; anchored to sandy holdfasts by byssus (silky filaments produced by mollusks for the purpose of attaching themselves to solid objects); often recovered by dredging and dragnet fishing (×⅔).

214. *Corculum cardissa* (L.), throughout the tropical area of the Pacific from the Philippines→southern Japan→Micronesia→ Melanesia, New Guinea→north and northwestern Australia; fairly common in sandy sublittoral zone among corals (×1).

215. *Strombus (Conomurex) luhuanus* L., in the Pacific islands from east-central Japan→the Philippines→Indonesia→Micronesia→ eastern Australia→Melanesia and as far as Palmyra Island; rather common everywhere in herds from the low-water mark to 20 m on sandy and gravelly bottoms with detritus associated with corals and rich in algae (×1).

214

215

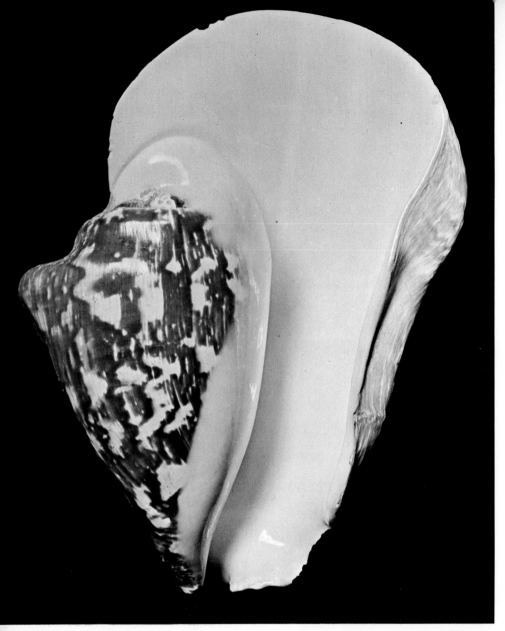

216

216. *Strombus (Tricornis) latissimus* L., in the Pacific islands from northern Ryukyu Islands, Japan→Taiwan→the Philippines→ Melanesia; not very common, beyond the reef edge on slightly sloping coral-sandy bottoms, around 4 to 15 m (×1).

217

217. *Strombus (Doxander) vittatus japonicus* Reeve, a Japanese subspecies, from central-southern Honshu→southern Kyushu; related to the typical form *S. vittatus vittatus* L., found from Hong Kong→southern China→the Philippines→the Gulf of Siam→New Guinea→the Great Barrier Reef and as far as Fiji; and to the other subspecies *S. vittatus campbelli* Griffith and Pidgeon, from northern to southeastern Australia; all fairly common in the west and south Pacific islands in herds on mud and muddy detritus from 2 to 60 m (×2⅓).

218

218. *Cymbiola* (*Aulica*) *aulica* (Sowerby), found only in a short stretch of sea of around 500 km in the Pacific from Sibuguey Bay, Mindanao, to the Tapul group of the Sulu Archipelago; fairly rare, on sandy bottoms from 4 to 45 m ($\times 1\frac{1}{3}$).

219   220

219. *Mitra cardinalis* (Gmelin), in the Pacific islands from southern Ryukyu Islands, Japan→the Philippines→Micronesia→ Melanesia→Polynesia→northern Australia, also found in the Indian Ocean from central eastern Africa→South India→Malay Peninsula; not very common and rare locally in coral-sandy circumlittoral zone from 40 to 60 m and below (×1⅓).

220. *Conus* (*Leptoconus*) *ammiralis* L., in the Indo-Pacific islands from the Kii Peninsula, Japan→the Philippines→Sulu Archipelago (particularly common here)→the Moluccas→the Great Barrier Reef→New Caledonia (unconfirmed records in the Seychelles); fairly common in the crevices of coral reefs (×2¼).

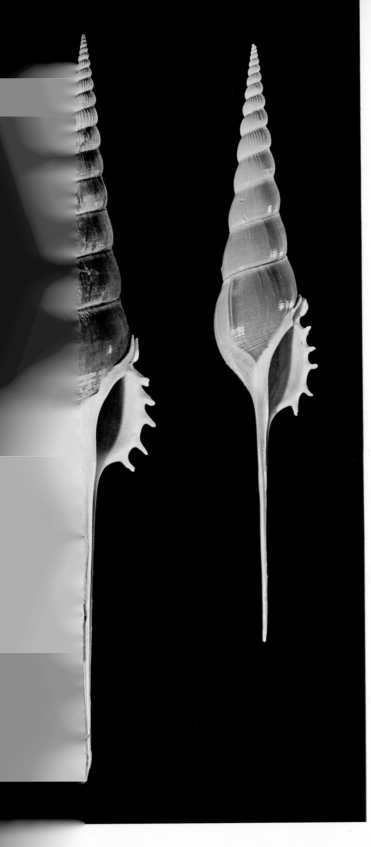

221. *Tibia fusus* L., in the Pacific islands from Taiwan→the Philippines→Indonesia→Melanesia; not very common, in sandy, muddy sublittoral zone from 20 m and below; with and without a periostracum (×⅘).

222. *Lambis* (*Millepes*) *millepeda* (L.), in the Pacific islands from Luzon, Philippines→Madura, Java→Timor→ northwestern New Guinea; not very common, in shallow water down to 4 m (×1½).

223. *Bursa* (*Gyrineum*) *rana* (L.), in the Pacific islands from central southern Honshu, Japan→the Philippines→ Micronesia→Melanesia as far as northern Australia; common in sandy sublittoral zone rich in algae from 20 to 100 m (×1).

223

224. *Haustellum haustellum* (L.), in the Pacific islands from southern Kyushu, Japan→the Philippines→New Guinea→ Fiji→northern Australia→India (recorded also in the Red Sea and in central East Africa); fairly common, usually in pairs, in muddy, sandy circumlittoral zone from 9 to 50 m ($\times$1).

225. *Murex tribulus* L., in the Pacific islands from southern Japan→the Philippines→New Guinea→northern Australia→ Fiji; common on coral bottoms from 35 to 60 m and below. A very variable species, related to synonymic forms such as the more typical Philippine *M. nigrospinosus* Reeve and the eastern *M. ternispina* Lamarck, recorded in the Red Sea and on the Malabar Coast ($\times$⅗).

224

225

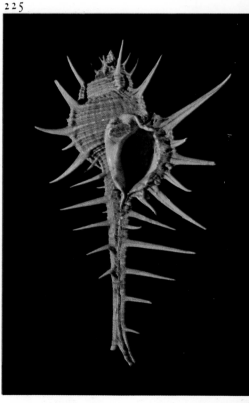

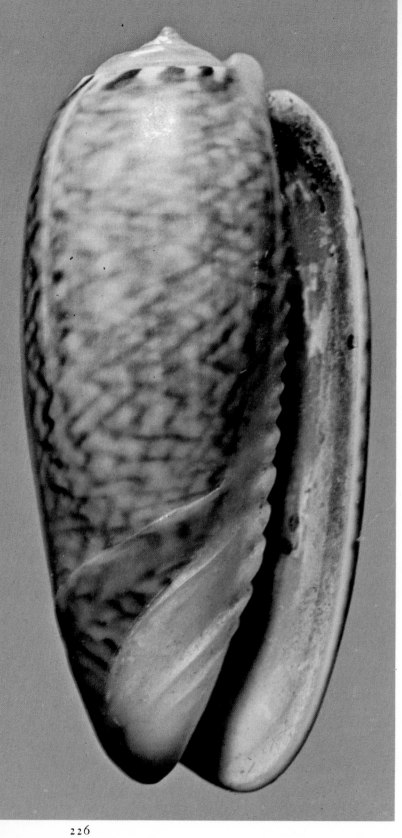

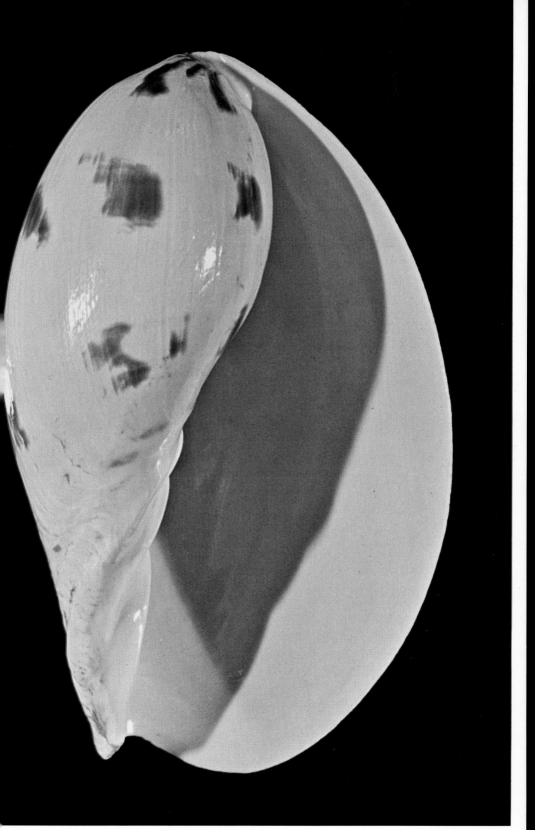

226. *Oliva* (*Carmione*) *mustellina* Lamarck, in the Indo-Pacific from the Bay of Bengal→Singapore and Indonesia→southern China→southern Shikoku, Japan→the Philippines→the Moluccas; fairly common on sandy coasts just beyond the lower midlittoral zone ($\times 3\frac{1}{2}$).

227. *Melo melo* (Lightfoot), in the Asiatic Indo-Pacific from Coromandel, India→Palk Bay, Sri Lanka→Malay Peninsula, Singapore→northern Borneo→southern China→Taiwan; not common, on muddy littorals from 0.50 to 10 m ($\times 1$).

228. *Melo* (*Melocorona*) *aethiopicus aethiopicus* (L.), in the Indo-Pacific islands of Indonesia, where detailed data on habitat are not recorded, while in the Philippines and northwest New Guinea *M. aethiopicus broderipii* Griffith and Pidgeon is fairly common from the low-water mark to 10 m on sandy, muddy bottoms; the example shown is of a gerontic (aged) specimen, which, having long passed the prime of life, had ceased to produce the typical crown of spines ($\times \frac{3}{4}$).

229

229. *Ficus subintermedius* (d'Orbigny), in the
Pacific islands from southern Honshu, Japan→the
Philippines→the Moluccas→New Guinea→
northwestern Australia and as far as New South
Wales, also recorded in South Africa; common in
sublittoral zone from 10 to 100 m; often brought
back by lobstermen (×1).

230

230. *Conus (Cylindrus)* *canonicus* Hwass in Bruguière, in the Indo-Pacific islands from Pangani, central East Africa→Indonesia→ Melanesia→Micronesia→Polynesia and as far as northeastern Australia; a fairly rare form, in coral sublittoral zone, very closely related to *C. textilis* (*see Fig. 155*) (×2½).

253

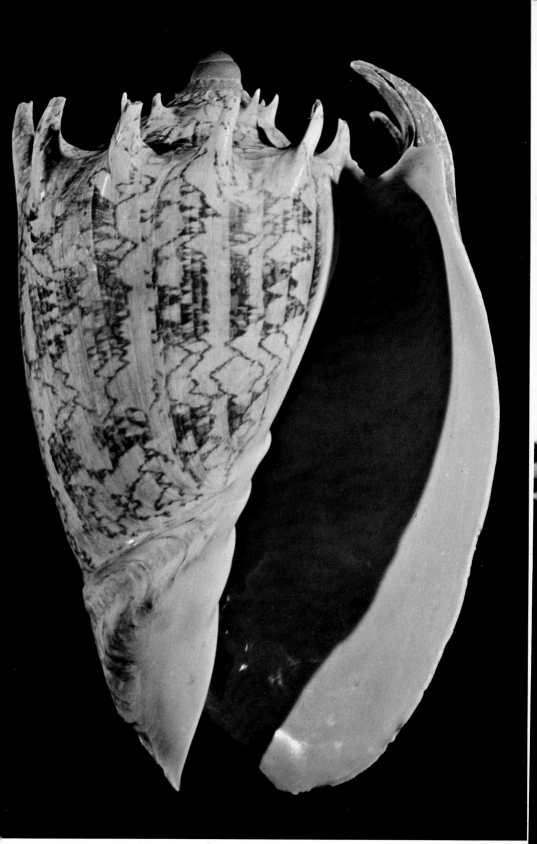

231. *Cymbiola (Aulica) imperialis* Lightfoot, found in a limited area in the Pacific islands of the Sulu Sea, in an arc of a few hundred kilometers from Mindanao to the Sulu Archipelago; not very common, on sandy bottoms from 2 to 20 m; the example shown belonged to an aged specimen ($\times \frac{5}{6}$).

Tibia

256

THE INDO-PACIFIC OCEAN

Australia

Australia's northeast and eastern parts lie in the Pacific Ocean, and its northwest, western, and southern parts in the Indian Ocean. In its Pacific Ocean zones, as we have seen, it shares the great faunistic richness of the Indo-Pacific, while its Indian Ocean zones have less widely distributed, more localized species, many of which are endemic or specifically Indian or South African. The Great Barrier Reef is in many ways a zoogeographic phenomenon. It is a gigantic habitat that is mostly homogeneous for a stretch of more than 2,000 kilometers; it is rich in biological communities, including shell-bearing animals with very specialized forms resulting from close interrelationships.

232

232. *Volutoconus bednalli* (Brazier), in the
Arafura Sea off northern Australia, centered
on Port Darwin; rather rare, in sandy
sublittoral zones from 8 to 45 m, more often
brought back by pearl fishers ($\times 1\frac{1}{4}$).

233

233. *Cymbiolista hunteri* Iredale, in eastern
Australia in a coastal arc 900 km long from
Newcastle, New South Wales→Moreton
Island, southern Queensland; fairly common
in sublittoral and circumlittoral zones from 20
to 150 m; recovered by dredging.

234. *Fusinus colus* (L.), form *longicauda* Lamarck, in northeastern Australia, frequent off the Great Barrier Reef and adjacent zones, from 5 to 65 m and below; part of a group widely distributed throughout the central Pacific and Indian oceans (×1 ¼).

235. *Livonia mammilla* (Sowerby), in southern and eastern Australia from the Great Australian Bight→ Victoria→northern Tasmania→ New South Wales and as far as Queensland; not common, in circumlittoral zone dredged up from 90 to 180 m (×¾).

234

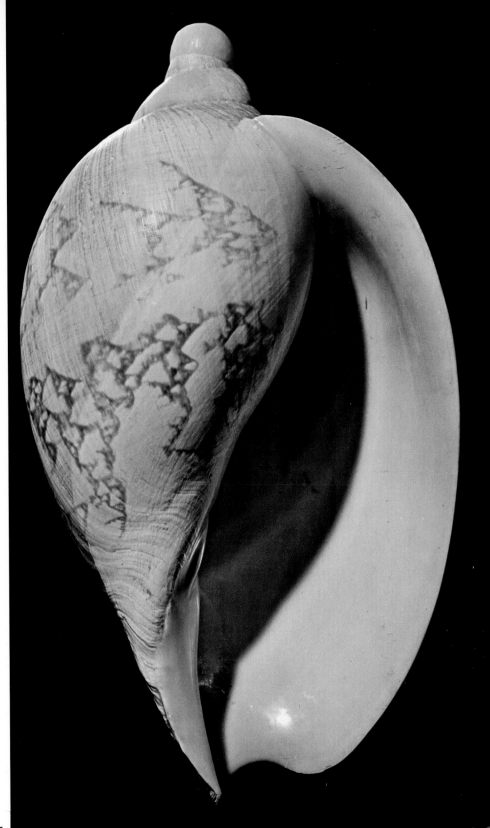

236

237

236. *Tellinota albinella* (Lamarck), in
southern Australia and Tasmania; not very
common, in sandy midlittoral and sublittoral
zones (×1¼).

237. *Pharaonella pharaonis* Hanley, in
Australia from Queensland to northeastern
Australia; common in sandy sublittoral zone
with algae (×1).

238. *Bassina disjecta* (Perry), in eastern and
southern Australia from New South Wales to
Victoria→Tasmania; not common, in lower
midlittoral zone and below, on muddy
sandbanks (×1¼).

238

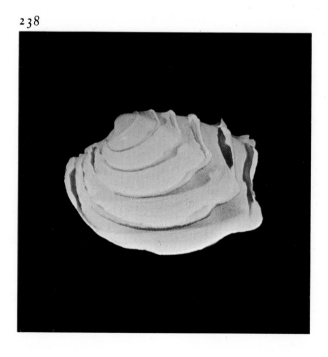

241

ON THE PREVIOUS PAGES:

239. *Ancilla* (*Ancillista*) *cingulata* (Sowerby in Broderip and Sowerby), in eastern Australia from New South Wales to Queensland; moderately common in sublittoral zone on bottoms populated with lobsters (×3).

240. *Bursa* (*Tutufa*) *bubo* (L.), in Australia along the Great Barrier Reef→Queensland; not rare, in sublittoral zone on coral rocks and gravels from 10 to 50 m; the species has a number of variant forms widely distributed in the Indo-Pacific from East Africa→the Laccadive Islands→Japan→Micronesia→Melanesia (×1).

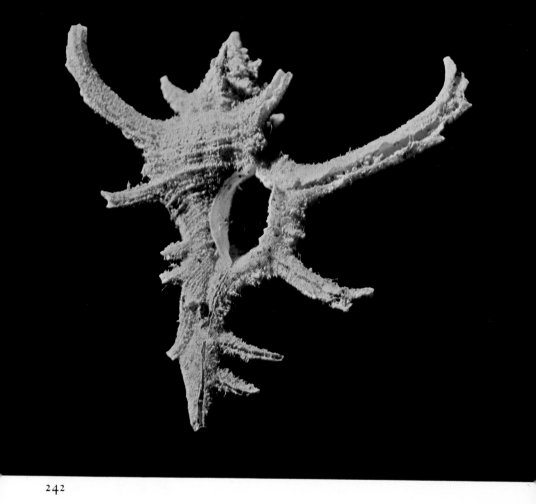

242

241. *Zoila friendii friendii* (Gray), in southwestern Australia from the Great Australian Bight off Eucla→Geographe Bay→ Dorre Island; not common, in sublittoral zone from shallow water to 200 m; feeds on sponges (×1⅖).

242. *Chicoreus axicornis* (Lamarck), in northern Australia, Queensland, and the Great Barrier Reef, but present as far as Indonesia, Japan, and South Africa (Natal); not common, on coral bottoms down to 100 m (×2¼).

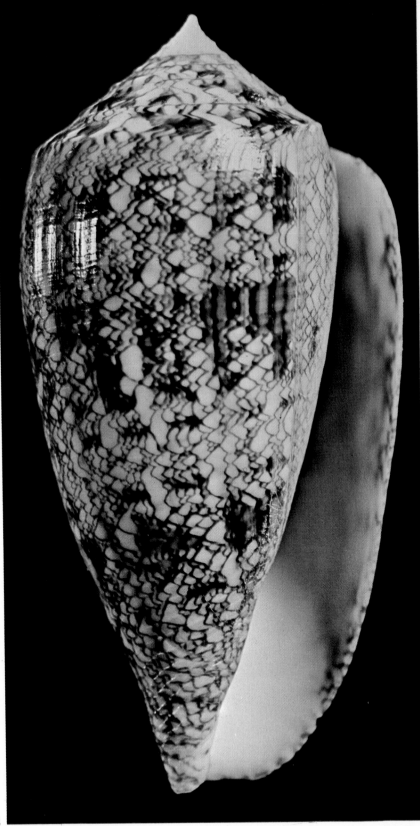

243

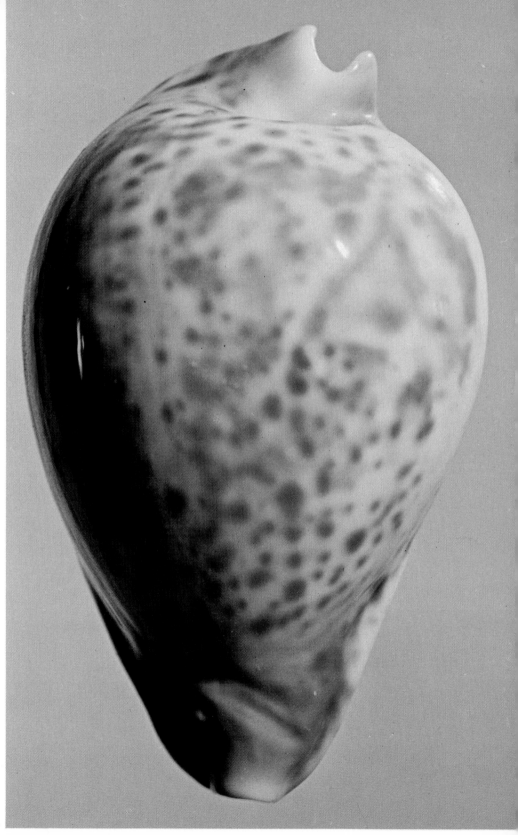

44

243. *Conus* (*Cylindrus*) *victoriae* Reeve, in northern and northwestern Australia; not common, in sublittoral zone in rock crevices and niches among madrepores ($\times 3\frac{1}{2}$).

244. *Umbilia hesitata* (Iredale) ♀, in southeast and southern Australia from New South Wales off Newcastle→off Victoria→Bass Strait, King Island, and as far as northern Tasmania; fairly common in circumlittoral zone and beyond, dredged up from 100 to 300 m and below ($\times 3\frac{1}{8}$).

245. *Penion* (*Austrosipho*) *maxima* (Tryon), in southern Australia (and along New South Wales) →Tasmania; not very common, in circumlittoral zone; picked up by dragnet fishing or in lobster pots ($\times \frac{3}{5}$).

246. *Maurea cunninghami* (Griffith and Pidgeon), in New Zealand; more common off western open-ocean sandy beaches with seaweed, from 15 to 50 m ($\times 1\frac{1}{6}$).

245

246

Fusinus

272

THE PACIFIC OCEAN, AMERICAN COASTS

Just as the West Indies (*see p. 137*) are the richest area in shell-bearing animals on the Atlantic side of the Isthmus of Panama, so on the Pacific side the richest region is between San Diego, in southern California, and Ecuador. The distribution of the fauna is considerably influenced by peculiar, variable hydrogeographic conditions. These are bound up with the interaction of horizontal surface tides and the vertical rise of abyssal ones, which affect the temperature at various levels, producing sudden changes that make it difficult for the majority of shell-bearing animals to live much below 100 meters. This explains why, in a zone that is bathed by the Pacific Ocean, the fauna has more in common with the fauna on the other side of the isthmus than with the fauna of the Indo-Pacific.

247

247. *Muricanthus ambiguus* (Reeve), on American Pacific coast from southern Mexico→Panama; common in sublittoral zone in shallow and moderately deep water rich in bivalves; this is an "intermediate" species from which two others separate: in the north, *M. nigritus* (Philippi) of Baja California, and in the south, *M. radix* (Gmelin) of Panama→southern Ecuador (×1⅙).

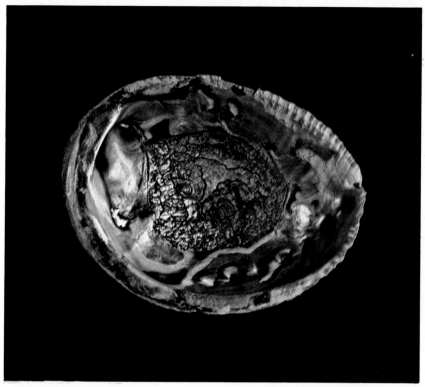

248

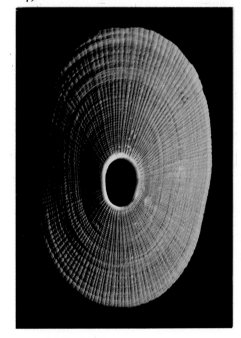

249

248. *Haliotis* (*Sanhaliotis*) *fulgens* Philippi, on American Pacific coast from the Channel Islands (California)→Baja California→northern Mexico, common in lower midlittoral zone and just below on rocks rich in vegetation (×½).

249. *Megathura crenulata* (Sowerby), on American Pacific coast from Monterey, California→Cedros Island, Baja California, Mexico; common in lower midlittoral zone on rocks, breakwaters, and jetties (×1).

250

250. *Pteropurpura trialata* (Sowerby), on American Pacific coast, along northern California and Baja California; common in sublittoral zone in moderately deep water rich in bivalves (×1⅙).

251. *Hexaplex erythrostomus* (Swainson), on American Pacific coast from the Gulf of California→Peru; very common just below the low-water mark and in sublittoral zone; feeds on bivalves (×⅘).

251

ON THE FOLLOWING PAGES:

252. *Hexaplex brassica* (Lamarck), on American Pacific coast from Guaymas, Baja California→Peru; rare in lower midlittoral zone, sporadically more common in sublittoral zone around 55 m, on beds of other mollusks ($\times 1\frac{1}{4}$).

253. *Oliva incrassata* Lightfoot, on American Pacific coast from Baja California, throughout the Gulf of California→San Felipe, Mexico→Peru; fairly common below the low-water mark and just beyond on sandy shores ($\times 3\frac{1}{2}$).

252

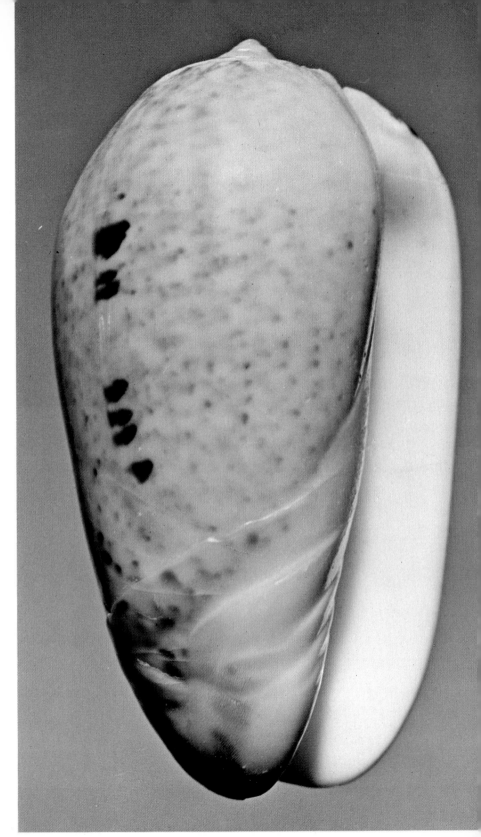

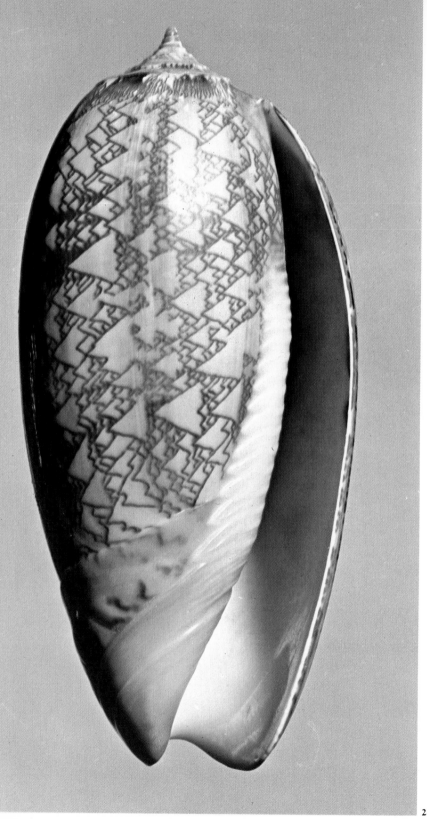

ON THE PREVIOUS PAGES:

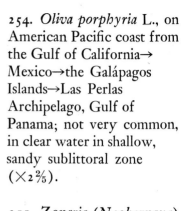

254. *Oliva porphyria* L., on American Pacific coast from the Gulf of California→ Mexico→the Galápagos Islands→Las Perlas Archipelago, Gulf of Panama; not very common, in clear water in shallow, sandy sublittoral zone (×2⅖).

255. *Zonaria (Neobernaya) spadicea* (Swainson), on American Pacific coast from Monterey Bay, California→ Cedros and Guadalupe islands; fairly common from lower midlittoral zone among seaweed, under rock ledges, and on muddy flats down to 45 m (×3).

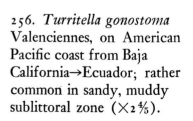

256. *Turritella gonostoma* Valenciennes, on American Pacific coast from Baja California→Ecuador; rather common in sandy, muddy sublittoral zone (×2⅘).

257. *Conus princeps* L., on
American Pacific coast from Gulf
of California→Ecuador; common
in midlittoral zone on rocky coasts
($\times 1\frac{1}{2}$).

257

258. *Conus* (*Cylindrus*) *lucidus*
Wood, on American Pacific coast
from Baja California→Ecuador;
fairly common in sublittoral zone
in shallow water on coarse sand
($\times 1\frac{1}{3}$).

258

259. *Fusitriton oregonensis oregonensis* (Redfield), on American Pacific coast from the Bering Sea→San Diego, California, and in the eastern Pacific from Kamchatka→ Hokkaido, Japan→northern Honshu, Sagami Bay; the subspecies *F. oregonensis galea* Kuroda and Habe is found in southern Japan from southern Honshu→Shikoku; not very common, on rocks and gravel in sublittoral zone, frequently picked up offshore by dragnets from 100 to 500 m ($\times 1\frac{4}{5}$).

260. *Hysteroconcha lupanaria* (Lesson), on American Pacific coast from Bahía Ballenas along Baja California→Peru, common on sandy shores from 0 to 24 m; it corresponds to the *H. dione* (*see Fig. 132*) found on the other side of the Isthmus of Panama ($\times 2$).

260

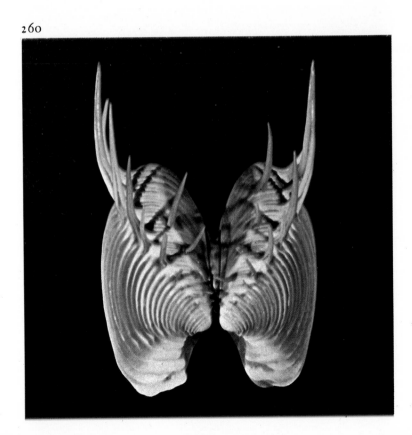

261

261. *Argopecten circularis circularis* (Sowerby), on American Pacific coast from Cedros Island, Baja California→ Paita, Peru; not common, in quiet sandy and muddy sublittoral zone; northward, as far as Santa Barbara, California, is found the fairly uncommon subspecies *A. circularis aequisulcatus* (Carpenter) (×2).

PART 3

Collecting Shells

WHERE AND HOW
TO COLLECT THEM

On-the-spot Research

The habitats indicated in the previous chapters are themselves an answer to the question "Where do you find shells?" But it is worth knowing a little more about the littoral species that can be easily gathered either on foot on the shore or by diving with a snorkel mask. It should also be borne in mind that the zones we have been dealing with are classifications made to facilitate human understanding and that nature is not obliged to respect them at all times.

To Collect, Not Merely Accumulate

A scientific collection, aimed at covering the whole range of species, should, if possible, include only specimens taken alive, and not shells inhabited by other animals (such as hermit crabs, which often take refuge in seashells), or already empty and cast up on the beach by the surf. An exception to this rule would be, of course, a very beautiful or uncommon specimen, but even in this case the value of the shell is diminished by this kind of provenance.

The situation is similar when an animal has been dislodged from its usual habitat by a rough sea and is collected fairly "fresh," though dead or dying, and with the flesh still within the shell; or when a shell is retrieved from the stomach of a predatory fish. In both cases, though the species may be particularly rare, the way in which the shell was found is abnormal and such shells are of limited scientific value.[1]

[1] *The number of shells found stranded and their density per square meter depends on the position of the respective colonies when alive, the direction of the wind and the movement of the waves, the tides, the season of the*

According to the normal, approved procedure, the collector should first procure or at least consult (for example, at the nearest harbor master's office) a table of the tides to determine the place of research and the times when the littoral area to be explored will be most exposed.

Another problem in collecting is how to carry off the material found. Small glass tubes, test tubes, and jelly jars are useful; polythene plastic bags have proved ideal, as they are waterproof, light, and unbreakable.

It is a good idea to use either plastic or stainless steel tweezers to pick up the smallest specimens. The bristles of an ordinary water-color paintbrush, dipped in water, are strong and delicate enough to pick up the tiniest (less than 5 mm), most fragile specimens.

According to your personal needs, or the time of the year, or the substrata on which you are working, you may need gloves, but it is better if you can do without them. The most suitable are rubber kitchen gloves, in which your fingers will still retain some feeling. Spades, rakes, hoes, and trowels are also used, and they are useful aids for someone who knows how to use them with the same care and to the same extent as an archaeologist on the track of precious ceramics. But the use of such tools generally leads to clumsy practices that are more likely to destroy specimens than to find them.

Sandy Beaches

On sandy beaches the best approach is to walk as far as possible along the lower tidemark, looking for signs of the tracks of species that creep or crawl, the small respiratory holes of siphons, the rhythmical movements and jet of water produced by species that

---

year, and the activity of underwater currents that turn out to be curiously selective, bringing only the right valves of certain bivalves into one area and taking the left valves somewhere else, perhaps without ever bringing them to the surface.

As for fish, the contents of their stomach are obviously of interest to ichthyologists as well, just as the shells inhabited by hermit crabs interest carcinologists.

live by filtering, and the humps and hollows of those that hide away almost completely buried. If you run your hand firmly under and across such tracks, with a little practice you should be able to grasp the prey if it is fairly large. To pick out smaller specimens, place handfuls of sand scooped up from the bottom in a sieve and rinse immediately in water.

Rocks

Collecting on rocks is a much more varied enterprise. You can look in cracks and crevices, poke about among algae and in pools, turn over the lighter stones and look underneath. (Be sure you put them back in their places.) Use a geological hammer carefully to dig out species that hollow out burrows in the rocks, and with an awl strip off the thin membranes of calcareous algae, a favorite home of young specimens.

Coral Reefs

The situation on coral reefs falls somewhere between the previous two. Many specimens can be collected by hand, others by exposing (with the help of an average-sized screwdriver) fronds of madrepores—which must be put back in place—at the base of which you will usually make some interesting finds.

Underwater

If you are proficient in underwater swimming, you will be able to explore the depths as well. Remember that if you want to move the sand, you need only agitate the water above it a little, and if you want to filter the sand, a tea strainer with your hand over the top will prove useful. To extract specimens from between rocks, try a chisel, using only your fist as a hammer.

Elsewhere

As has been pointed out, rather unusual places to look for shells are in the digestive organs of various fish and many starfish. It is not uncommon to find interesting shell-bearing animals there, and you should start by learning to recognize the fishes and starfish that prey on shell-bearers.

Tricks of the Trade

Obviously, expertise can come only from dealing with particular cases out in the field. Thus, if you take up shell collecting methodically and assiduously, experience will teach you that it is a good idea to number in advance the containers you intend to fill, using a thick pencil that will stand up to sea water and preservatives. In this way you will provide a handy link between your finds and the place where you found them, which will be important later on.

Other tricks of the trade include stretching a piece of nylon stocking across the bottom of a sieve to catch smaller specimens. Also run a strainer (made of plastic to be less destructive) through the tufts of algae as entomologists do with their nets through stands of foliage. This enables one to pick out tiny specimens that are hardly visible to the naked eye, or difficult to pick up in other ways.[2]

Finally, it should be mentioned that the majority of operations suggested here are better carried out at night with portable lighting.

Less adventurous collectors of shells can always fall back on the help of fishermen. In that case you must not wait on the quay to see what has been brought back[3] (specimens obtained in this man-

---

[2] *Profitable work on algae can be done on a table. Having uprooted and carried away a tuft of algae, put it in sea water in a transparent container and place it on a black or white surface. Leave it in darkness for a few hours, after which you will find that the tiny animals hidden in the tangle of weed will emerge, drawn toward the surface of the water in search of oxygen.*

[3] *When the catch is gutted and cleaned on board, try to obtain the intes-*

ner are comparable to those thrown up by storms). More often than not, you will be permitted to go on board the fishing boats in order to observe the catch, keeping an eye open for shells, and noting the zone, depth, and type of bottom from which they come.

This brings us to a very important point: from a scientific point of view, the value of a shell specimen depends mainly on the amount of specific information known about it from the very moment it is found.

Date and Place

These are both of fundamental importance to the collector. As far as the date is concerned, make a note of whether the find occurred during the morning, afternoon, evening, or nighttime, and obviously give the full date. In less than twenty-three years the great museums, where the best collections are finally deposited, will have specimens collected in three different centuries, so it is important to write "1977" and not just "77."[4]

The best way of indicating locality is as follows: for coasts, use the name adopted and recognized in U. S. Geological Survey maps, with the relevant map reading; for localities on the open sea, give the latitude and longitude, or better still, refer to nautical charts or naval maps. If you make a list of the zones to be visited in turn, you can give each a number and mark it on the various containers for the specimens found in each zone. This has the advantage of being practical and precise, as has already been suggested (*see p. 292*).

But, even more important, the technical geographical data should include an accurate description of the kind of habitat visited: if among rocks, whether the find was made in a pool or a crevice, or if exposed to the surf; if on the beach, whether in fine

---

tines of the largest fishes from some willing fishermen. The entrails often contain interesting shell-bearing animals and should not be thrown into the sea but put into a container with a suitable preserving fluid.

[4] *Those who have to deal with the collections in some of the oldest institutes today do not always realize when they are involved with objects that are a hundred or even two hundred years old.*

or coarse sand; if in estuary waters, in brackish lagoons, on the seabed, and so on.

Naturalists of the old school paid, and still pay, great attention to sea and sky conditions. The tide level at collecting time should be noted. The sky can be described as "calm," "overcast," "full of fleecy clouds," or "cloudy," but these are everyday rather than scientific terms. In both cases one is dealing with largely empirical evaluations that either correspond to exact measurements by light meters, current meters, anemometers, psychrometers, and the like, or are of little value.

From the biological point of view the microhabitat is important too. This refers to the smallest details of the environment in which the collected specimens lived and includes chemical analyses of the substratum and the associated animal and vegetable species, in addition to such information as: "under small calcareous stone covered with Bryozoa,"[5] "on *Ulva lactuca*,"[6] "on coral (algae) with *Halichondria panicea*,"[7] or "associated with *Dentalium vulgare*," and so on.

An Appeal

When looking for shells, the conchologist and malacologist should never forget that he or she is first and foremost a naturalist, not an obsessive collector of specimens. The indiscriminate removal of specimens can seriously damage the replacement of an animal population, particularly if it is a rare or very localized one. An appeal to students along these lines was made in a circular put out by the Unitas Malacologica Europaea in June 1972.

---

[5] *Animals with tentacles that form extensive, encrusting colonies.*

[6] *The "sea lettuce," a green algae (Chlorophyceae) common on stony bottoms in well-lit areas near the surface of calm water.*

[7] *Encrusting sponges.*

ARRANGING A
COLLECTION

The first step toward putting a collection of specimens into some kind of order is finding the best way of transporting them, and the most important point here is the interval of time involved.

If you happen to work on an oceanographic ship or in a marine biology laboratory, you will know what to do and have the means to do it. But if you have to take your specimens back to your own home, you will need to work out some plan of action. If you are not going back to base for a few days, you will need to use proper methods of preservation. Choose suitable containers and leave enough sea water in them to cover the animals. Then put in seven parts of industrial alcohol to three parts of sea water, a mixture that will slow down the process of decay for a fairly long period.[1] On the other hand, if you don't have far to go, it is better to keep the animals alive, so that you can then use better methods for disposing of them.

To keep the animals alive, it may seem quickest to leave them in containers with a little of their native water, but a small amount of water will become overheated and quickly lose its oxygen, while a lot of water will be too heavy and cumbersome to carry.

But as the specimens one sees in fish markets prove, shelled animals can survive for some time out of water, if they are kept in

[1] *In unusual conditions, where there are no facilities for preserving shell-bearing animals, they are kept alive by changes of water until arrival. The abundance of the catch sometimes makes it necessary to find a quick, simple way of storing them, and kerosene has proved very useful. The finest tissues dissolve in this in about fifty hours without giving off an unpleasant smell, and then need only rinsing in water to finish the job. The shells do not seem to be harmed by such emergency treatment, provided they are kept out of the liquid sediment that accumulates in the bottom of the drum.*

damp, well-aerated conditions. These can be provided by putting some wadding soaked in sea water into the smaller containers and some pieces of fresh-picked algae into the larger ones; the algae will help prevent the animals from being tossed about and, as we have seen, often harbor other species that will emerge in time. If you are doing the kind of research that requires undamaged specimens, you can use the sort of coarse shavings used as litter in bird cages and stables, or the ordinary straw used in packing crates, but first make sure that it has not been contaminated by any toxic substances. These materials, if soaked in water first, can preserve specimens as well as algae can. Keep specimens this way for periods of no more than twenty-four hours, particularly in summer, because beyond this limit even the algae may suddenly go bad, infecting and ruining everything.

For much longer journeys, it is a good idea to carry a reserve supply of sea water so that you can maintain the humidity of the containers en route. Occasionally open them for a change of air, unless you are using jelly jars fitted with gauze or nylon stocking lids.

When you reach base, the next problem is emptying the containers, which depends very much on what you intend to do next.

It is cruel and scientifically not advisable to kill the animal and remove its flesh from the shell by throwing it in boiling water or heating it in any way. Although it may be a good method from a gastronomic point of view (though not always for mollusks), cooking is not acceptable on a scientific level. As is well known, it causes a profound and irreversible transformation of the body tissues and seriously affects the small amount of protein in the shells; it brings about the immediate destruction of the periostracum and accelerates the various slow processes of decay, resulting in a milky opalescence of the colors and surface gleam that is soon followed by total calcination.

To avoid this, prepare some unaerated water (sea water, if dealing with marine species) by boiling it rapidly for twenty minutes and then cooling it in hermetically sealed containers. The majority of marine shell-bearing animals breathe through their gills, so if they are put into unaerated water they will die of asphyxiation; as their muscles slacken, they will easily come out of their shells. You can speed up the process a few minutes by adding drugs: the traditional ones are a 2 per cent solution of beta-eucaine (5 per cent) or chloral hydrate (7 per cent); more recent innovations are a 0.88 per cent solution of Nembutal and a 1 per cent solution of propylene phenoxetol.

A new, hitherto unpublished technique, which is particularly useful when dealing with small specimens, is floating some ordinary ice cubes in the half-full containers. As the ice melts and the sea water is gradually diluted, the asphyxiation of the animals is speeded up and the drop in temperature results in greater muscle relaxation.

Satisfactory results can also be obtained by putting the containers with the live animals in their native water in the freezer compartment of a refrigerator. When the liquid has solidified in its container, take it out, pour in just enough industrial alcohol to cover the frozen surface, and allow it to melt slowly.[2]

All the routines described are practical and fairly quick, and they serve to prepare the shells and their contents for scientific use. Certainly, if you abandon a scientific approach, you abandon everything: you provide no separate containers for each area and no notes, you leave the animals to die in the air and pull the flesh out bit by bit, or, if you have a garden, dump them in a corner and hand over the business of cleaning them to the wasps, beetles, scavengers, and ants, just as the big commercial exporters of shells do.

But if you want the shells to end up as serious scientific specimens, you won't want to put a lot of effort into collecting them and then treat them badly.

If you delay extracting the soft parts until after the muscles have relaxed, you should be able to get them out more easily, and you can either examine them immediately or preserve them for future examination. You can usually identify shell-bearing animals just by looking at their shells, but their proper classification always depends more on the fleshy parts. Here are found important anatomic features: the digestive, respiratory, and reproductive systems

---

[2] *In certain cases, with very quick deep freezers, the animals can be put right in and left for six, twelve, or up to seventy-two hours. The contraction of the soft parts helps to separate them from the inside walls of the shell without damaging it, but in typical gastropods it is only a useful beginning.*

so essential to proper systematic work. Thus it is useful to preserve the flesh of at least the less familiar specimens, which may require an expert to help identify them. In such cases it is ideal if you can preserve the whole animal without separating flesh from shell.

There are two basic methods of doing this: soaking in preservative liquid and drying.

For the former, use a 70 per cent solution of ethyl alcohol, but add it slowly, so that the tissues do not dry out too quickly; they should spend at least twenty-four hours and preferably seventy-two in a 30 per cent solution before being put into a 50 per cent[3] solution. In the latter case, the specimen is first soaked in a 40 per cent solution of isopropyl alcohol or in a 90 per cent solution of ethyl alcohol, for at least seventy-two hours but preferably twice as long. It is then placed on sheets of blotting paper (ordinary paper or newspaper is just as good) and left to dry in dark, dry surroundings for five to six days or as long as seems necessary. Then, when you need them, just soak the specimens in a solution of trisodium phosphate (5 grams per liter of water) and you will find that the muscles swell to almost their original size and the natural color pattern reappears.

It is essential to preserve the flesh of brachiopods and scaphopods, and also all the material found in the stomachs of fishes and starfish if these contain shells.

To remove the fleshy parts of shell-bearing animals, there is one method recommended for bivalves and another for gastropods.

Once the bivalve is open, all you need is a sharp penknife to cut off the adductor muscles where they are fixed to the valves (*see p. 13*); the rest of the flesh will then slide out. The remnants of the muscles can then be cleaned out with the point of the penknife or, if you prefer, with a histology lancet. Leave the ligament whole, because its elasticity lasts for some time after the animal is dead; it will not prevent you from examining the hinge and getting information from it.

---

[3] *You can also use a 7 per cent solution of Formalin, but to prevent the formaldehyde acting on the limestone of the shell, it must be neutralized with calcium carbonate. (The use of Formalin is not advised, as it may produce a serious allergic response in some people.)*

After examining the hinge, press the valves against each other in their normal position and wind some cotton thread around them. Leave the shell in a dark, aerated place so that the elastic ligament will stiffen as it dries and remain permanently closed.

Among the gastropods, limpets and such are not a problem, but it is not so easy to extract the fleshy parts from species with a high spiral shell from which they are not ejected by relaxation alone. The best method in such cases is to grasp firmly the part that protrudes with a pair of dental pliers and pull with a circular movement. If despite every precaution you find that some fragment remains inside, usually at the apex, a syringe made of rubber will help. Squirt firmly with lukewarm water, and the jet will usually manage to remove the last remains. If there is an operculum, it should not be disposed of but should be preserved together with the shell.[4]

Wash the specimen again in fresh water or industrial alcohol and leave it to dry in the dark; a suitable place is on a dish rack: this will allow any liquid left in to run out.

The next step is to find a safe and suitable home for your specimens. Unfortunately the majority of collectors, whether beginners or not, now carry out the kind of "cleaning" that is always harmful to the scientific value of the find. They want to get rid of the encrustations (often including the periostracum itself) that are such clear indications of the animal's way of life. They use detergents and corrosives, currycombs, scalpels, files, and who knows what else, and then varnishes, glues, lacquers, plastics, and so on.

The kind of person who boils shells will also file them and bedaub them, but a real naturalist will adopt a very different approach. If in its natural setting the shell was encrusted with sponges, algae, worm tubes, and Bryozoa—all unmistakable signs of its marine origin—cleaning it will obviously denaturalize it.

If, however, an incrustation seems to be particularly disfiguring,

---

[4] *If all the stages of preparation have been carried out correctly, the shell should not have any kind of smell. If there is a persistent smell, it can be removed with a few drops of one of those non-syrupy aromatic liqueurs traditionally used for cocktails, or with Formalin (diluted—see note 3), or, in really persistent cases, with a mixture of liquid paraffin. These are all better than using some other strong perfume.*

or the shell is to be displayed in a museum or photographed, you can remove the incrustation with the help of a steel needle without scratching the shell.[5] But it is not wise to do this to a single specimen of a species or to specimens that are rare in other ways.

The only kind of restoration worth attempting is protecting or repairing the protein part of the shell, which tends to wear out even when kept under the best conditions.

The traditional method is to polish the shell at three-year intervals with a soft cloth dipped in a little paraffin. This is enough to leave the shell covered with a little grease that may help it to resist inevitable organic decay.[6]

The chief cause of this decay is light, coupled with inadequate ventilation. This is why specimens shut up in airtight glass cases in museums often look so dull. Serious collections should be kept in drawers and not in airtight containers (*see diagram*).

Organization

A collection can be arranged on geographical, systematic, or environmental lines, or on a combination of all three. For example, once you have decided on the principles most suited to your material, you can begin to devote a drawer, or a section, or whatever, to a particular environment, such as "rocky shores." This would then contain all the specimens found in such a setting; they should not be put in at random but grouped together in boxes or given different colored labels according to their geographical provenance and systematic category.

This kind of sophisticated and painstaking organization is also the most natural. It can, in fact, be set up without any real knowledge of classification, which can even be an advantage; all you need do is pay attention to your ecological and geographical notes, which can be made without any serious study, and then you can add the determinations (names) at a later date. Even without

---

[5] *If you know how to use it, a dentist's drill is definitely recommended.*

[6] *Baby oil has proved particularly good for maintaining natural colors.*

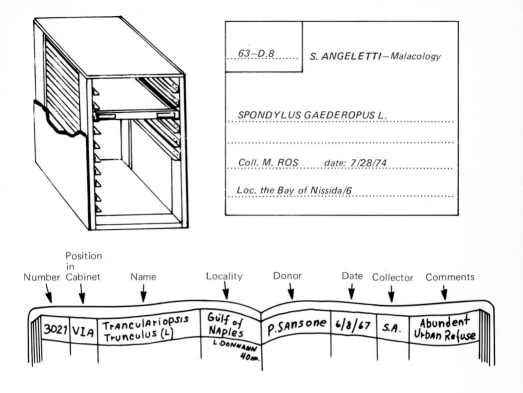

them, if you have arranged your collection carefully it will have considerable scientific value and can easily be consulted by people used to the proper scientific approach.

A popular method of organization is based on areas of distribution such as the Mediterranean and the central Pacific. These are then subdivided according to the system of classification described in the "Systematic Notes." You can obviously insert the determinations into the geographical structure and vice versa, but if you put the determinations first,[7] the significance of the environment can be overlooked.

Whatever method of organization you decide on, it is most important that every collection be scientifically labeled so that each specimen can be identified and characterized.

As your specimens start to accumulate, give each a number in a

[7] *As is done, however, in almost all traditional museum collections.*

262

262. *Nautilus pompilius* L., (*see also Figs. 4 and 208*); when young, this specimen had a traumatic shock, probably as a result of being bitten by a predator (fish, turtle, and so on) that damaged the mantle, which then produced an extensively "scarred" shell; until the beginning of this century this single pathological specimen would have been enough to authorize the creation of a new species ($\times \frac{4}{5}$).

special register (*see facsimile*) and note down the exact date of the finds—including who found them—and, where possible, their scientific name and who identified them, and also their position in the drawers, once you have established it. All this information should have a place on the labels (*see facsimile*) of the individual boxes and tubes.

After a while, as the collection grows, a card index of the species contained in it will prove very useful. It is better not to wait until the moment when you actually need it, or you will find yourself having to attempt a major task in far too much of a hurry, as well as having to work out the scientific names of all the specimens (*see* "*Systematic Notes,*" *p. 19*). On your index of the species you should indicate the area of distribution, habitat, any notable characteristics, and then bibliographical references—above all, those from magazines and bulletins that do not have general indexes—personal observations and comments from other collectors, and finally the identification numbers of the examples in your collection.

Precautions

While shells should be protected from light, they should not be kept in airtight containers, to prevent the formation of mold. This rule applies to all specimens, not only those with a periostracum, which are likely to be attacked by the larvae of *Dermestes* beetles, which feed on cuticular tissues. If the drawers are opened (in darkness) from time to time and a few moth balls are kept in them, this should provide adequate protection, but if any symptoms of spoilage occur, or seem likely to occur, they can be dealt with by spraying the drawers with a concentrated solution of carbolic acid in alcohol.[8]

[8] *Using all the precautions such a powerful poison demands.*

Reference Notes

BIBLIOGRAPHY

ABBOTT, R. T.

1960. "The genus *Strombus* in the Indo-Pacific," *Indo-Pacific Mollusca*, Vol. I. Philadelphia.

1961. "The genus *Lambis* in the Indo-Pacific," *Indo-Pacific Mollusca*, Vol. I. Philadelphia.

1968. "The Helmet Shells of the World," *Indo-Pacific Mollusca*, Vol. II. Philadelphia.

1974. *American Seashells.* 2d ed. New York.

ALLAN, J.

1950. *Australian Shells.* Melbourne.

1956. *Cowry Shells of the World Seas.* Melbourne.

ANGELETTI, S.

1968. *Conchiglie da collezione.* Novara.

1971. "Conchiglie," *Il Mare*, Vol. III. Novara.

1973. "Molluschi," *Il Mare*, Vol. VI. Novara.

1977. *Conchiglie—Raccolta e Collezione.* Novara.

ANGELETTI, S., and MELONE, G. C.

1968. "Su alcune Mesalie rinvenute recentemente nel Tirreno," *Conchiglie*, Vol. IV. Milan.

BARLETTA, G.

1969, 1972. "Malacofauna del Mar Rosso," *Conchiglie*, Vols. V, VIII. Milan.

BIGGS, H. E. J.

1965. "Mollusca from the Dahlak Archipelago, Red Sea," *J. Conch.*, 25.

1972. "Report on the Marine Mollusca collected by the British Dahlak Quest Expedition, Red Sea, 1969–1970," *J. Conch.*, 27.

BOMBACE, G.

1969. *Appunti sulla malacofauna e sui fondali circalitorali della penisola di Milazzo.* Palermo.

BOUSFIELD, E. L.

1964. *Coquillages des côtes canadiennes de l'Atlantique.* Ottawa.

BOWDEN, J., and HEPPEL, D.

1968. "Revised List of British Mollusca," *J. Conch.*, 26.

BROST, F. B., and COALE, R. D.

1971. *A guide to Shell Collecting in the Kwajalein Atoll.* Rutland, Vt., and Tokyo.

BURGESS, C. M.

1970. *The Living Cowries*. New York and London.

CATE, C. N.

1966. "Philippine Cowries," *The Veliger*, 8.

1968. "Western Australian Cowries: a second, revised, and expanded report." *The Veliger*, 10.

1969. "The Eastern Pacific Cowries," *The Veliger*, 12.

1969. "The Cowrie Species Living at Guam," *The Veliger*, 12.

CERNOHORSKY, W. O.

1967, 1972. *Marine Shells of the Pacific*. Vols. I (rev. 1971), II. Sydney.

1970. "Systematics of the families Mitridae and Volutomitridae," in *Bull. Auckland Inst. Mus.*, No. 8.

1976. "The Mitridae of the World," *Indo-Pacific Mollusca*, Vol. III. Greenville, Del.

CHAVAN, A.

1966. *Les Mollusques et leur détermination*. Paris.

CONCI, A., and GHISOTTI, F.

1966. *Conchiglie*. Milan.

COTTON, B. C.

1957. *Australian Recent and Tertiary Species of Mollusca*. Pamphlet issued by Royal Society of Southern Australia. Adelaide.

CROWSON, R. A.

1970. *Classification and Biology*. London.

DANCE, S. P.

1974. *The Encyclopedia of Shells*. London.

DEAS, W.

1971. *Seashells of Australia*. Adelaide.

DUFFUS, J. H.

1969. "Associations of Marine Mollusca and Benthic Algae in the Canary Island of Lanzarote," *Proc. Malac. Soc. Lond.*, 38.

EKMAN, S.

1967. *Zoogeography of the Sea*. London.

FRETTER, V., and GRAHAM, A.

1962. *British Prosobranch Molluscs*. London.

GHISOTTI, F., coll.

1964. *Schede Malacologiche del Mediterraneo*. Milan.

GHISOTTI, F., and MELONE, G. C.

1970–. "Catalogo illustrato delle conchiglie marine del Mediterraneo," *Conchiglie*, Vol. VI–. Milan.

GOETTING, K. J.

1974. *Malakozoologie*. Stuttgart.

GRAHAM, A.

1971. *British Prosobranch and other operculate Gastropod Molluscs.* London and New York.

HABE, T.

1964. *Shells of the Western Pacific in Color.* Vol. II. Osaka.

HIRASE, S., and (TAKI, I.).

1954. *An Illustrated Handbook of Shells from the Japanese Islands and Adjacent Territory.* Tokyo.

HORNELL, J.

1951. *Indian Molluscs.* Bombay.

KEEN, A. M.

1971. *Sea Shells of Tropical West America.* 2d ed. Stanford, Calif.

KENNELLY, D. H.

1964. *Marine Shells of Southern Africa.* Johannesburg.

KENSLEY, B.

1973. *Sea Shells of Southern Africa: Gastropods.* Cape Town.

KIRA, T.

1965. *Shells of the Western Pacific in Color.* Vol. I. 2d ed. Osaka.

KURODA, T., HABE, T., and OYAMA, K.

1971. *The Sea Shells of Sagami Bay (collected by His Majesty the Emperor of Japan).* Tokyo.

LUBET, P., and AZOUZ, A.

1969. "Etude des Fonds chalutables du Golfe de Tunis," *Bull. Inst. Oceanogr. Pêche Salammbô,* I.

MC MILLAN, N. F.

1968. *British Shells.* London.

MARCHE-MARCHAD, J.

1958. *Nouveau catalogue de la collection de Mollusques testacés marins de l'IFAN.* Dakar.

MARSH, J. A.

1964. *Cone Shells of the World.* Brisbane and Sydney.

MORTON, J., and MILLER, M.

1968. *The New Zealand Sea Shore.* London and Auckland.

NICKLES, M.

1950. *Mollusques testacés marins de la Côte occidentale d'Afrique.* Paris.

NORDSIECK, F.

1968. *Die Europäischen Meeres-Gehäuseschnecken.* Stuttgart.

1969. *Die Europäischen Meeresmuscheln.* Stuttgart.

1972. *Die Europäischen Meerensschnecken.* Stuttgart.

1972. "Marine Gastropoden aus der Shiqmona-Butcht in Israel," *Arch. Moll.,* 102.

PARISI, V.

1966. "Nuovi sviluppi di ricerca sulla Filogenesi dei Molluschi," *Lav. Soc. Malac. Ital.*, Vol. III.

1970. "I popolamenti delle acque costiere ed estuariali," in *Quad Civ. Staz. Idrob. Mil.*, I.

PENNIKET, J. R.

1970. *New Zealand Seashells in Colour.* Wellington.

PORTER, H. J., and TYLER, J.

1971. *Sea Shells Common to North Carolina.* Morehead City, N.C.

POWELL, A. W. B.

1973. "The Patellid Limpets of the World," *Indo-Pacific Mollusca*, Vol. III. Greenville, Del.

PURCHON, R. D.

1968. *The Biology of the Mollusca.* (Also 2d ed., 1977.) Oxford.

RADWIN, E., and D'ATTILIO, A.

1976. *Murex Shells of the World.* Stanford.

REHDER, H. A.

1973. "The Family Harpidae of the World," *Indo-Pacific Mollusca*, Vol. III. Greenville, Del.

RIPPINGALE, O. H., and MC MICHAEL, D. F.

1961. *Queensland and Great Barrier Reef Shells.* Brisbane.

ROSEWATER, J.

1965. "The Family Tridacnidae in the Indo-Pacific," *Indo-Pacific Mollusca*, Vol. I. Philadelphia.

SALVINI-PLAWEN, L. VON.

1968, (1969). "Solenogastres und Caudofoveata (Mollusca, Aculifera): Organisation und philogenetische Bedeutung," *Malacologia*, 9: *Proc. Third Europ. Malac. Congr.* Vienna and Ann Arbor, Mich.

1970. "Muscheln," Chaps. I, VII in *Enzyklopädie des Tierreiches*, Vol. III. Zurich.

SCHILDER, F. A.

1969. "Repertorium der Radulae der Triviacea und Cypraeacea," *Arch. Moll.*, 99.

SCHILDER, F. A., and SCHILDER, M.

1938. "Prodrome of a monograph on living Cypraeidae," *Proc. Malac. Soc. Lond.*, 23.

SETTEPASSI, F.

1970. *Atlante Malacologico: Molluschi marini viventi nel Mediterraneo.* Vol. I. Rome.

SMYTHE, K. R.

1972. "Marine Mollusca from Bahrain Island, Persian Gulf," *J. Conch.*, 27.

SORGENFREI, T.

1962, (1965). "Some Trends in the Evolution of European Molluscan Faunas," *Proc. First Europ. Malac. Congr.* London.

SPRY, J. F.

1961. "The Sea Shells of Dar es Salaam: Gastropods," *Tanganyika Notes and Records,* No. 56 (rev. and expanded, 1968).

1964. "The Sea Shells of Dar es Salaam: Part II, Pelecypoda (Bivalves)," *Tanganyika Notes and Records,* No. 563.

STARMÜHLNER, F.

1968. "Investigation about the Mollusc Fauna in Submarine Caves," *Proc. Symp. Moll. India,* Part I.

1968, 1969. "Zur Molluskenfauna des felslitorals bei Rovinj (Istrien)," *Malacologia,* 9: *Proc. Third Europ. Malac. Congr.* Vienna and Ann Arbor, Mich.

TEBBLE, N.

1966. *British Bivalve Seashells.* London.

THORSON, G.

1962, (1965). "The Distribution of Benthic Marine Mollusca along the N. E. Atlantic Shelf from Gibraltar to Murmansk," *Proc. First Europ. Malac. Congr.* London.

TINKER, S. W.

1958. *Pacific Sea Shells.* 2d ed. Rutland, Vt., and Tokyo.

TORCHIO, M.

1964. *Biologia marina.* Milan.

1968. "Elenco dei Cefalopodi del Mediterraneo con considerazioni bio-geografiche ed ecologiche," *Ann. Mus. Civ. St. Nat., Genova,* 77.

1969. "Le Coste del mare: flora e fauna," *Enc. della Natura,* I. Rome.

1969. "I Cefalopodi attuali," *Gli Animali e il loro mondo,* 101. Milan.

1971. "Lo studio dei Molluschi prima che la Natura muoia," *Natura,* 62.

1972. *La vita nel mare.* Novara.

TURK, S. M.

1973. *Concordance to the Field Card for British Marine Mollusca.* London.

VILAS, C. N., and VILAS, N. R.

1970. *Florida Marine Shells.* Rutland, Vt., and Tokyo.

VOKES, E. H.

1971. "Catalogue of the Genus *Murex* Linné," *Bull. Amer. Paleont.,* Vol. LXI.

WARMKE, G. L., and ABBOTT, R. T.

1961. *Caribbean Seashells;* Narberth, Pa.

WEAVER, C. S., and DU PONT, J. E.

1970. *Living Volutes.* Greenville, Del.

WENZ, W.

1938, 1944. "Gastropoda: Prosobranchia," *Handbuch der Paläozoologie.* Berlin.

WILSON, B. R., and GILLETT, K.

1971. *Australian Shells.* Sydney.

WILSON, B. R., and MC COMB, J. A.

1967. "The Genus *Cypraea* (subgenus *Zoila* Jousseaume)," *Indo-Pacific Mollusca,* Vol. I. Philadelphia.

ZILCH, A.

1959, 1960. "Gastropoda: Euthyneura," *Handbuch der Paläozoologie.* Berlin.

PHOTOGRAPHIC CREDITS

ALDO BALLO, Milan: 187, 193, 233.

GIORGIO BARLETTA, Milan: 91.

CARLO BEVILACQUA, Milan: 1, 3, 5, 6, 7, 8, 10, 11, 12, 13, 15, 16, 18, 20, 22, 23, 25, 26, 27, 28, 29, 30, 31, 32, 33, 34, 35, 39, 43, 44, 45, 46, 50, 51, 52, 54, 56, 59, 60, 61, 62, 63, 64, 65, 67, 68, 69, 70, 71, 78, 80, 81, 82, 83, 85, 87, 92, 93, 94, 95, 96, 97, 98, 99, 100, 101, 102, 103, 104, 107, 108, 109, 110, 111, 121, 128, 129, 132, 133, 135, 136, 137, 138, 139, 141, 142, 143, 144, 145, 146, 147, 150, 151, 152, 160, 161, 162, 163, 164, 165, 166, 168, 169, 170, 171, 175, 176, 177, 178, 180, 181, 182, 183, 184, 185, 186, 190, 191, 192, 194, 195, 196, 197, 200, 201, 202, 203, 205, 206, 207, 208, 213, 214, 215, 216, 217, 218, 221, 222, 226, 229, 230, 231, 232, 235, 239, 240, 241, 242, 243, 244, 247, 253, 254, 255, 262.

MARCO FERRARIO, Milan: Frontispiece, 117, 118, 120, 122, 123, 124, 125, 126, 130, 252, 256, 257, 258, 259.

GIOVANNI PINNA, Milan: 2, 9, 14, 21, 37, 38, 40, 41, 49, 58, 66, 72, 73, 74, 79, 84, 105, 112, 113, 114, 115, 116, 119, 127, 131, 134, 140, 148, 149, 153, 154, 156, 157, 158, 159, 167, 172, 173, 174, 179, 188, 189, 198, 199, 204, 209, 210, 211, 212, 219, 220, 223, 224, 225, 227, 228, 234, 236, 237, 238, 245, 246, 248, 249, 250, 251, 260, 261.

MARIO ROSIELLO, Naples: 17, 19, 24, 36, 42, 48, 53, 55, 57, 75, 76, 77, 86, 88, 89, 90, 106.

The photographs by G. Pinna belong to the collection of the Civic Museum of Natural History, Milan.

The numbers above refer to plates rather than pages.

BIOGRAPHICAL
NOTES

Sergio Angeletti is an internationally known conchologist and a voluntary assistant at Milan's Civic Aquarium and Hydrobiological Station. He was born at Jesi, in the Marches, on 11 January 1943, but the following year his family moved to Milan, where he still resides.

His interest in the natural world, and above all in zoology, began when he was very young. At age six, he had already started a collection of Coleoptera, under the tutelage of the entomologist Mario Tomassetti, who was a friend of the family. At age twelve, he started collecting shells, and by the time he had graduated from the Liceo Parini he had decided to devote his life to malacology. He studied at the University of Milan's Institute of Zoology and was given the task of reorganizing the nomenclature of the entomological and malacological collections preserved there.

In 1964, at the age of twenty-one, he received a grant from the National Research Center to carry out research on the malacological fauna of the Gulf of Naples at the Naples Zoological Station, where he again worked as a guest researcher in 1966 on a series of histochemical and pharmacological studies of various characteristic species of mollusks. In 1974 he began, at the Naples Zoological Station, his present work, the systematic revision of the Mediterranean bivalve mollusks.

After having specialized in malacology, Professor Angeletti left the University of Milan in 1967 and that year became a member of the Società Malacologica Italiana (and was a member of their delegation to the Third European Malacological Congress at Vienna in 1968); he also became a member of the Deutsche Malakozoologische Gesellschaft, the Malacological Society of London, the Conchological Society of Great Britain and Ireland, the Unitas Malacologica Europaea, the Conchological Society of Southern Africa, and the Société Française de Malacologie. He is a fellow of the Società Italiana di Scienze Naturali and in 1975 was appointed as coordinator of the Regional Scientific Group of the World Wildlife Fund.

Professor Angeletti has written for various professional publications, advised on the *Vocabolario Illustrato della Lingua Italiana* (*The Illustrated Dictionary of the Italian Language*) by Devoto and Oli (1967) and in 1965 wrote the book *Conchiglie da collezione*, published by the Istituto

Geografico de Agostini (1968). He collaborated on the *Il Mare* encyclopedia, also published by the IGDA. Aside from his professional publications,
Professor Angeletti has written widely for popular illustrated magazines and
newspapers and has appeared at numerous conferences and interviews, and
on radio programs.

He has also contributed extensively to the reorganization of the shell
collection of the Civic Museum of Natural History in Venice.

INDEX

319

333